MOUNTAIN B

IN

THE PEAK DISTRICT

20 Circular Routes In And Around The National Park

By

DAVE MASON B.Sc.(Hons) C.Eng. MIEE

Dedicated to my son, Paul.

BRIDESTONE BOOKS

ACKNOWLEDGEMENTS

My thanks to all those who have helped me in the compilation of this book; in particular:

The Peak Planning Board for the use of their definitive maps to check the routes.

Ian Tucker and Charles Johnson for their assistance with the photography.

Paul Durber and Peter Carley for their assistance with computer technology.

My wife Susan for checking the manuscript.

ABOUT THE AUTHOR

Dave Mason is a chartered engineer living in Congleton on the western fringe of the Peak District. A keen fell walker for over twenty years, he was introduced to mountain biking by his son and now enjoys the pleasures of both pursuits equally. He has used his extensive knowledge of the Peak District, gained from many years of walking the area, to compile a set of mountain bike trails encompassing the finest scenery and most interesting places in the National Park.

NOTE

Every effort has been made to ensure that the routes are open to mountain bikes. However, neither the author nor publishers accept responsibility for parts of the trails that may be closed to cyclists.

Published by Bridestone Books
12, Lindale Close, Congleton, Cheshire. CW12 2DG

Printed by Deanprint Limited, Cheadle Heath, Stockport SK3 0PR.

First Edition - June 1991
Reprinted - October 1991
Second Edition - January 1992 - Minor amendments to Trails 3 and 13
Reprinted - May 1992
Third Edition - October 1992 - Minor amendments to Trails 5 and 8

CONTENTS

	Page
INTRODUCTION	1
PREPARATION	4
OVERALL LOCATION MAP	6
THE TRAILS:	
1 - CHATSWORTH FROM MONSAL HEAD	7
2 - THE EYAM CIRCUIT	14
3 - WIN HILL	21
4 - THE HIGH PEAK CIRCUIT	25
5 - GOYT VALLEY	31
6 - LADYBOWER	38
7 - THE TISSINGTON CIRCUIT	43
8 - THREE SHIRE HEADS AND LUD'S CHURCH	49
9 - THE MATLOCK CIRCUIT	56
10 - THE UPPER DOVE VALLEY	64
11 - MAM TOR AND EDALE	69
12 - THE MANIFOLD CIRCUIT	75
13 - AXE EDGE MOOR	82
14 - THE ROACHES FROM DANEBRIDGE	87
15 - WILDBOARCLOUGH AND MACCLESFIELD FOREST	93
16 - THE CLOUD	100
17 - RUDYARD LAKE	105
18 - MIDDLEWOOD WAY AND LYME PARK	109
19 - THE LONGNOR CIRCUIT	114
20 - THE MERMAID AND MORRIDGE	118

INTRODUCTION

Mountain biking is a new and exciting sport that has rapidly established itself as one of the premier outdoor pursuits. Mountain bikes are great fun and have added a new dimension to cycling. Their low gearing and rugged construction enable the exploration of remote locations that have previously been inaccessible to cyclists. They allow cyclists to go off-road, away from the traffic and fumes of today's busy roads into the wide open spaces, fresh air and scenery.

The aim of this book is to maximise your pleasure from mountain biking by describing 20 circular trails through some of the finest countryside in England - the Peak District National Park. The trails have been selected for their scenic beauty and places of interest. Some of the region's fascinating history has also been included to further enhance your enjoyment.

The trails follow bridleways, rough tracks and minor roads and are generally unsuitable for ordinary bikes. They start from car parks for the convenience of cyclists who transport their bikes by car, yet they are circular so you can start from any point.

The trails are graded into three categories - easy, moderate and difficult. The easy trails present no real difficulties while the moderate trails have short sections of rough terrain. The difficult trails have extended sections of rough terrain.

The routes range from 15 to 50 kilometres (10 to 33 miles). All are strenuous but can be completed by anyone with a reasonable level of fitness. Easy-to-follow, step-by-step instructions are provided with clear maps showing the route and points of interest. Distances are given in kilometres (kms). Multiplying by 2 and dividing by 3 gives the approximate equivalent mileage.

Every effort has been made to ensure that the routes used are open to mountain bikes. However, an increasing number of 'No Cycling' signs are appearing. If you encounter signs prohibiting cycling or objections from landowners, comply with their requests and find an alternative route. If you inform the publishers I will incorporate changes in subsequent editions.

There has been some animosity between mountain bikers and walkers. This largely arises, it has to be said, from inconsiderate behaviour by mountain bikers such as riding past walkers at high speed, braking hard behind them or failing to give way and forcing walkers off the track. When approaching walkers you should slow down and shout "excuse me". This alerts the walkers to your presence and they will usually make room for you to pass. As you pass the walkers don't forget to thank them or exchange a few pleasantries. By observing these simple rules of common courtesy mountain bikers and walkers can share the countryside in a spirit of peace and harmony.

Mountain bikes are criticised for causing track erosion. Bikes are not the only contributors to this problem; walkers and horses cause their share and the worst offenders are scramble bikes and off-road vehicles which have destroyed the surface of many tracks. You can take a few simple precautions to reduce the problem:

a) Always stay on the track, don't use the grass alongside

b) Avoid heavy braking unless absolutely necessary

c) Don't ride over grass in wet weather

The countryside is there for our enjoyment and that of future generations. Help to preserve it by observing the Country Code:

Guard against fire risks

Fasten all gates

Keep dogs under control

Keep to paths across farm land

Avoid damaging fences, hedges and walls

Leave no litter

Safeguard water supplies

Protect wild life, plants and trees

Go carefully on country roads

Respect the life of the countryside

PREPARATION

Many of these trails will take you miles from civilisation, so the following are notes on the equipment you will need and checks you should make before you set off.

Clothing:
Choose clothing suitable to the weather conditions. Shorts and teeshirt may seem adequate for the warm summer months but the weather is notoriously changeable, particularly in the hills. You should always carry a cagoule. In winter months you will need a warm jacket and pair of trousers or leggings. Always wear brightly coloured clothing or a fluorescent band.

There is a very real danger that you may fall and crack your head. You should, therefore, always wear a helmet. The modern lightweight helmets are comfortable to wear and give excellent protection. Specialists footwear is available but a stout pair of trainers is normally adequate.

Equipment:
These trails are unsuitable for ordinary cycles. You will need a Mountain or All Terrain Bike (A.T.B.). These bikes are specially strengthened to withstand the rigours of off-road cycling. Mountain bikes vary considerably in price and quality. You will need to select your bike according to personal preference and budget. The minimum specification is a sturdy frame, 15 gears, 50mm. tyres with reinforced rims and cantilever brakes.

Over rough terrain the possibility of punctures increases. You will need to carry a puncture repair kit, pump, spanners and tyre levers. A spare innertube will also save time and trouble and doesn't take up much space. The directions for these trails are easy to follow but you should carry a map and compass in case you get lost. It is also a good idea to carry a whistle in case of real emergencies.
A number of the trails include excursions to points of interest that can only be reached on foot. It is therefore useful to carry a lock and chain so that you can secure your bike to the nearest post or tree. Many of these trails pass places where you can buy refreshments but it is wise to carry a water bottle and some food. Also if there is a chance that you will be out after dark you should carry front and rear lights.

Checks:
Before you set out you should make the following checks:

Tyres - correct pressure, no splits or thorns etc.

Wheels - rims not damaged or buckled, bearings sound, spokes tight.

Frame And Forks - not cracked or damaged.

Gears - correctly adjusted and lubricated.

Chain - correctly adjusted and lubricated.

Brakes - pads not excessively worn, correctly adjusted and cables not frayed.

Lights - good working order.

Reflectors - clean and undamaged.

If any of the above checks reveal problems you should repair or replace the item before setting off. Having sorted out the above you are now ready for the trail.

!ENJOY YOUR BIKING!

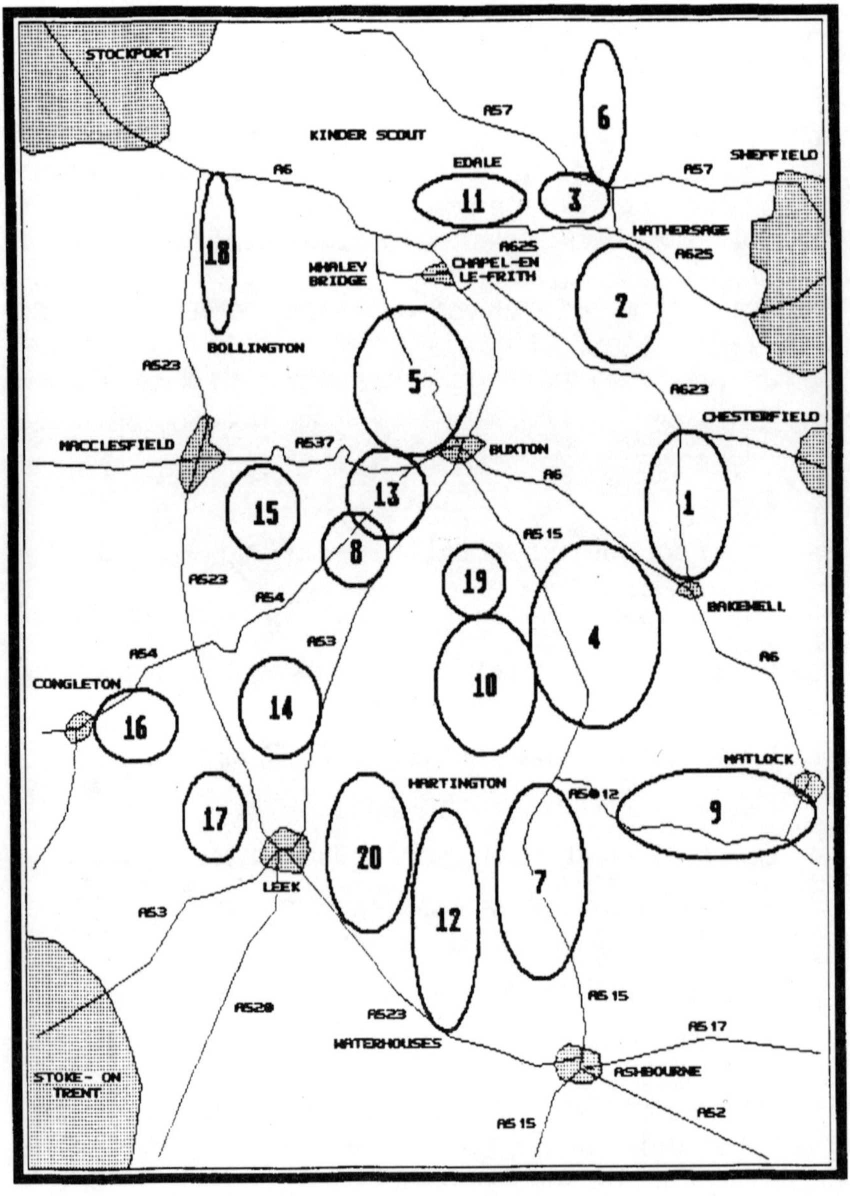

OVERALL LOCATION MAP

TRAIL 1 - CHATSWORTH FROM MONSAL HEAD

Distance: 27 kilometres (18 miles)

Terrain: Hilly, rough tracks, minor roads and a short stretch of main road.

Grading: Moderate.

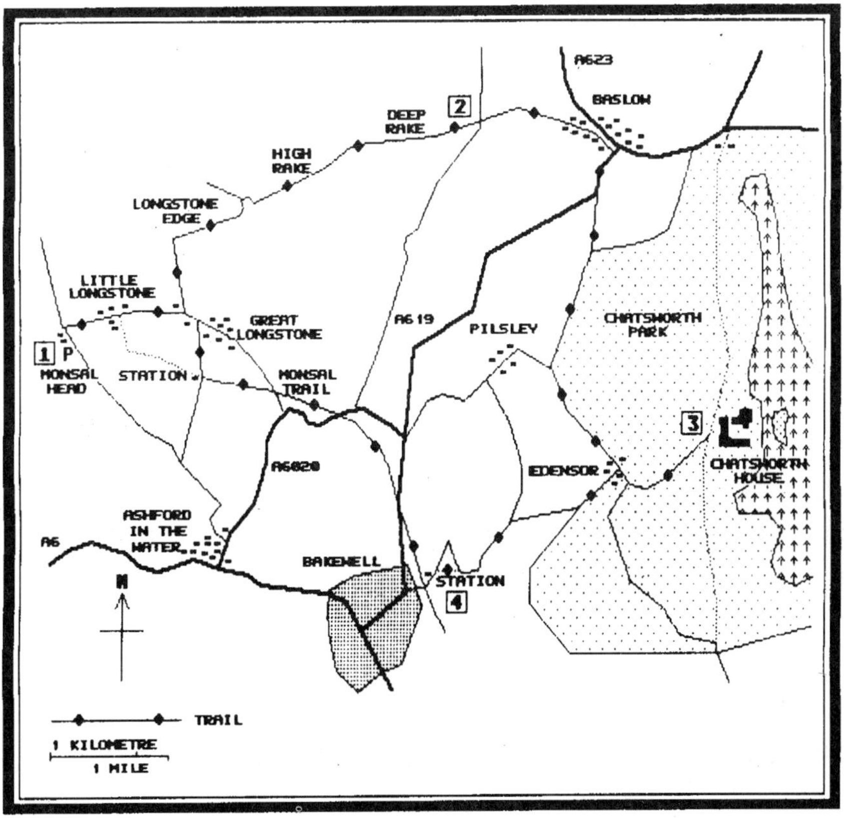

Home of the Duke and Duchess of Devonshire, Chatsworth is one of the finest stately homes in England. Set in a lush valley by the banks of the river Goit and surrounded by wooded hills, the house and its grounds make a magnificent sight. The grounds were designed by Capability Brown and feature waterfalls and fountains fed by gravity from a man made lake on the hill behind the house. The famous Emperor Fountain spouts a column of water up to ninety metres into the air.

The route also encompasses the dramatic limestone edges above Great Longstone, the picturesque villages of Baslow and Edensor and a section of the scenic Monsal Trail.

POINT 1

Our starting point is a beauty spot in its own right. Monsal Head overlooks Monsal Dale one of the most picturesque valleys in Derbyshire. Turn north off the A6 Bakewell to Buxton road at Ashford In The Water and follow the signs for Monsal Head. There is a 'pay and display' car park at the rear of the Monsal Head Hotel.

POINT 1 TO POINT 2

Before you set off take some time to admire the views of Monsal Dale from the view point opposite the hotel. The viaduct that straddles the valley below once carried the Bakewell to Buxton railway.

Our route lies in the opposite direction on the road to Great Longstone. Follow the road downhill from Monsal Head passing through the village of Little Longstone. A km. further along on the outskirts of Great Longstone take a left turn to Longstone Edge by the village water pump.

The lane climbs steeply and bends to the right onto Longstone Edge. As you cross the Edge you will see panoramic views of the surrounding hills and valleys. Over to the west you can just distinguish Chatsworth Park in the distance. After a km. the road sweeps around to the left onto an open plateau. Turn right through a metal gate and cross a cattle grid. Follow the limestone track to your right over the hill onto High Rake.

The track crosses High Rake and Deep Rake with spectacular gorges on either side where fluorspar has been quarried from the limestone. From the end of Deep Rake the track descends steeply down a rough stone track to a road.

POINT 2 TO POINT 3

Cross the road to the lane opposite. Follow this lane through woods and farmland for about three kms. to the delightful riverside village of Baslow. As you enter the village the road runs alongside the river Goit. The river passes over a weir and under a delightful arched stone bridge that is over five hundred years old. Baslow is situated at the Northern end of Chatsworth Park but unfortunately there is no access for cycles at this point. It is however worth taking time to explore this charming village before continuing.

Leave the village by the Bakewell road and after a few hundred metres turn left on the road to Edensor, for three kms. As you enter the village you will see the church on your right and a little further along a road going off to your left. Follow this road down the hill and across an ornamental stone bridge to Chatsworth House. As you descend the hill the house and gardens make an incomparable sight.

Take time out to explore the house and gardens - you will not be disappointed.

Chatsworth House

Chatsworth has a long history. The first house was built by Bess of Hardwick and her second husband Sir William Cavendish in 1552. This formidable lady was married four times and accumulated a fortune in the process. She befriended Mary Queen of Scots during her captivity at Chatsworth.

She was briefly imprisoned in the tower of London when Queen Elizabeth I suspected her of conspiring with Mary. All that remains of this era is the hunting tower on the hill behind the house and the ruins of Queen Mary's Bower close to the bridge.

The current house was started by the Duke of Devonshire in 1687 and has been extended and improved by his ancestors since that time. The gardens were designed by Lancelot 'Capability' Brown and feature an enormous variety of shrubs and trees, a 200 metre water cascade, waterfalls, a bronze tree that spouts water from the tips of its branches, a yew maze and of course the magnificent Emperor Fountain.

POINT 3 TO POINT 4

When you have completed your exploration of Chatsworth, retrace your route up the road to Edensor. Turn left by the church and keeping it on your left follow the lane up through the village.

Edensor is a charming collection of decorative stone buildings and carefully tended gardens. The church is raised on a mound in the centre of the village and is a marvellous sight in the spring when it is surrounded by daffodils.

As you leave the village the lane gives way to a rough track that climbs the hill to a minor road. Turn left and continue up the hill. If you look to your right you will see High Rake and Deep Rake that you crossed earlier. Over the brow of the hill, watch out for a bridleway going off to your left, just before Ballcross Farm. The entrance to the bridleway is across a low stone wall by a gate. Descend steeply through the trees for a km. to meet a minor road by a golf course. Below you is the splendid town of Bakewell.

Turn left down the hill and at the bottom of the hill you will cross a disused railway line. This is now the Monsal Trail. If you wish to explore Bakewell turn left into the town. Otherwise, turn right and after a few hundred metres right again into the car park at the front of the old Bakewell Station.

POINT 4 TO POINT 1

The entrance to the Monsal Trail is at the left hand side of the station. Turn left along the trail and follow it for approximately five kms. through pleasant woodland and open countryside. When you reach Great Longstone Station (now a private residence) leave the trail at the bridge and turn left along a lane for a km. to Great Longstone. Turn left by the Crispin Inn and follow the road around to the left towards Little Longstone. Follow the road up through Little Longstone back to the finishing point at Monsal Head.

TRAIL 2 - THE EYAM CIRCUIT

Distance: 21 kilometres (14 miles)

Terrain: Hilly, rough tracks and minor roads.

Grading: Moderate.

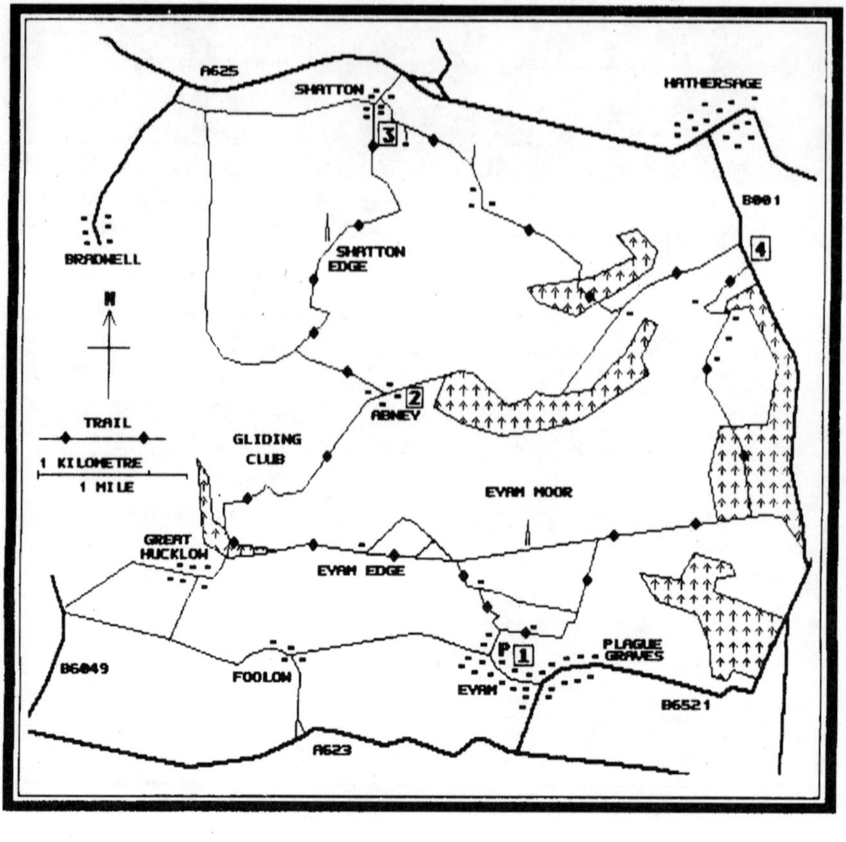

This trail starts and finishes in the fascinating village of Eyam. A congregation of pristine buildings built from pale yellow sandstone, this beautiful village belies it's tragic history. Eyam was one of several places in the north of England to be ravaged by the bubonic plague.

It started in September of 1665 when George Viccars, a lodger with widow Mary Cooper, took delivery of a bolt of cloth from London where the 'Black Death' was rife. The cloth was damp and was spread out to dry.

It is believed that fleas from the cloth infected the inhabitants. Within days the death toll was increasing rapidly and the Rector William Mopesson persuaded the villagers to quarantine the whole village.

Food and medical supplies were left at agreed points around the village and paid for with money left in vinegar, to act as disinfectant. Over a period of fourteen months the plague exacted its terrible toll, killing 259 of a population of 350.

Church services were held in the open air and victims were buried close to their homes to prevent the spread of infection. Names of victims are painted on plaques outside many of the houses and William Moppeson's register of the deaths can still be seen in the church. The Riley graves on the east side of the village contain the remains of no less than seven members of the Hancock family buried by their mother.

A macabre relic of the plague era is the children's nursery rhyme:

Ring a ring o'roses
A pocket full of posies
A-tishoo A-tishoo
We all fall down

The ring o'roses was the rash that was the first symptom of the disease. Posies were herbs carried in the pockets to counteract the infection, a-tishoo represents sneezing, another symptom and the rest of the rhyme describes the terrible consequences.

Eyam has many other points of interest that makes it extremely popular with tourists. In August each year there is a sheep roast in the centre of the village on an ornate mechanical spit. Also in August is the well dressing ceremony and a procession to Cucklet Delf where services were conducted by William Mopesson during the plague years.

Opposite the gates to Eyam Hall, on a small green, are the village stocks and down the hill adjacent to the traffic island is a metal plate set in the surface of the lane. Under the plate is a bull ring used for the barbaric practice of bull-baiting. The bull was chained to this ring and dogs were set upon the unfortunate beast until it was savaged to death.

Eyam has been supported by many different industries over the years. In the eighteenth century, lead mining on nearby Hucklow Edge was a primary source of income. Cotton spinning also contributed greatly to the relative prosperity of the area and supported two mills.

By the nineteenth century the mines were depleted and competition from water powered mills had decimated the cotton industry. Silk weaving was introduced by Ralph Wain who had invented a process for weaving a pattern on both sides of the cloth. The same process was sold to the silk mills in Macclesfield and demonstrations of the technique can still be seen in the Macclesfield Silk Museum.

Eyam later became a centre for shoe making but this has declined over the years and the community now relies on tourism, agriculture and quarrying. A small museum in the centre of the village gives a further insight into this intriguing place and is well worth a visit.

Riley Graves - Eyam

The trail completes a circuit of Abney and Eyam Moors providing some of the finest views in the Peak District from the Eyam and Shatton Edges.

POINT 1

To reach Eyam village turn north off the A623 to the east of Stoney Middleton. After half a km. you will arrive in the centre of Eyam. Follow the signs to the car park on the west side of the village.

POINT 1 TO POINT 2

From the car park turn right up the hill for three hundred metres to where a lane marked with a 'dead end' sign goes off to your left. The enthusiasts amongst you should take this lane. It is steep, rutted and strewn with boulders but great fun. Lesser mortals may wish to continue along the road and take the next left turn to Great Hucklow. These alternative routes converge near Highcliffe farm.

Follow the road west towards Great Hucklow. The road turns right and then left onto Eyam Edge. To the north is the prospect of Eyam Moor, dominated by a towering radio mast. To the south are uninterrupted views towards Tideswell and beyond. This undulating country, latticed with limestone walls, makes a superb vista that stays with you for three kms. as you traverse the length of the edge. Half way along the edge you will pass the Barrel Inn. Ignore the left turn to Foolow and continue towards Great Longstone.

On the outskirts of the village, take a right turn for Abney. The road passes through a small wood and emerges opposite the Derbyshire And Lancashire Gliding Club. Ideally sited on a flat topped hill, the runway is surrounded by the elongated trailers used to transport gliders. On most weekends you will see several of these graceful craft swirling in the thermals rising from the surrounding hills.

When you are ready to continue, follow the road around the gliding club and down a hill to the hamlet of Abney.

POINT 2 TO POINT 3

The approach to Abney is via a delightful wooded dell. A short climb up the other side brings you to the centre of the hamlet. On your right you will notice an old fashioned red phone box, one of the few that hasn't been replaced by the modern shower cubical version. Turn left into a lane opposite the phone box and proceed for about one km. to where the lane becomes a rough track and divides in two. Take the right fork heading towards the summit of Shatton Moor. At the base of the summit the track swings sharply to the left and after a few hundred metres turns right through a gateway onto Shatton Edge.

As you follow the track along the hillside, the views are absolutely stunning. Starting near Castleton a string of peaks - Mam Tor, Hollins Cross, Lose Hill and Win Hill - enclose the fertile Hope valley. Further along the track, the massive Ladybower dam comes into view to the right of Win Hill. From this angle the huge volume of water suspended high above the valley is an awe-inspiring sight. Continue along the track past a radio mast and descend the hill for one and a half kms. to the hamlet of Shatton.

POINT 3 TO POINT 4

As you enter Shatton you will pass a road on your left which fords a stream. Two hundred metres further along take the lane to your right by a white house that has a stone mushroom in the garden. The lane bends right and left and arrives at a gate where the lane turns right up the hill towards Westfield Farm. Carry straight on through the gate along a cart track for one and half kms.

This is a most pleasant stretch of track running across the meadows on a hillside above the river Derwent. Further along, the cart track rises and then drops to a gate, where it intersects with a limestone track. Turning right, the track climbs steadily and leads onto a metalled lane. Follow the lane around to the left for one km. dropping down through the woods and up to a junction with a minor road. Turn left and follow the road downhill for two kms. to a junction with the B6001 opposite the Plough Inn.

POINT 4 TO POINT 1

Turn right along the road for two hundred metres and turn right into a narrow lane. The lane climbs steadily through two hairpin bends and along the hillside for four kms. to a T-junction. Turn right up the hill for one and a half kms. The radio mast on Eyam Moor seen at the start of this comes into view and signals that you are close to the finish. Follow the road around to the left, along the top of the hill and drop down the other side through a wooded glade, back to the car park at Eyam and the finish of this trail.

TRAIL 3 - WIN HILL

Distance: 30 kilometres (20 miles)

Terrain: Hilly, rough tracks, minor roads and a short stretch of main road.

Grading: Difficult.

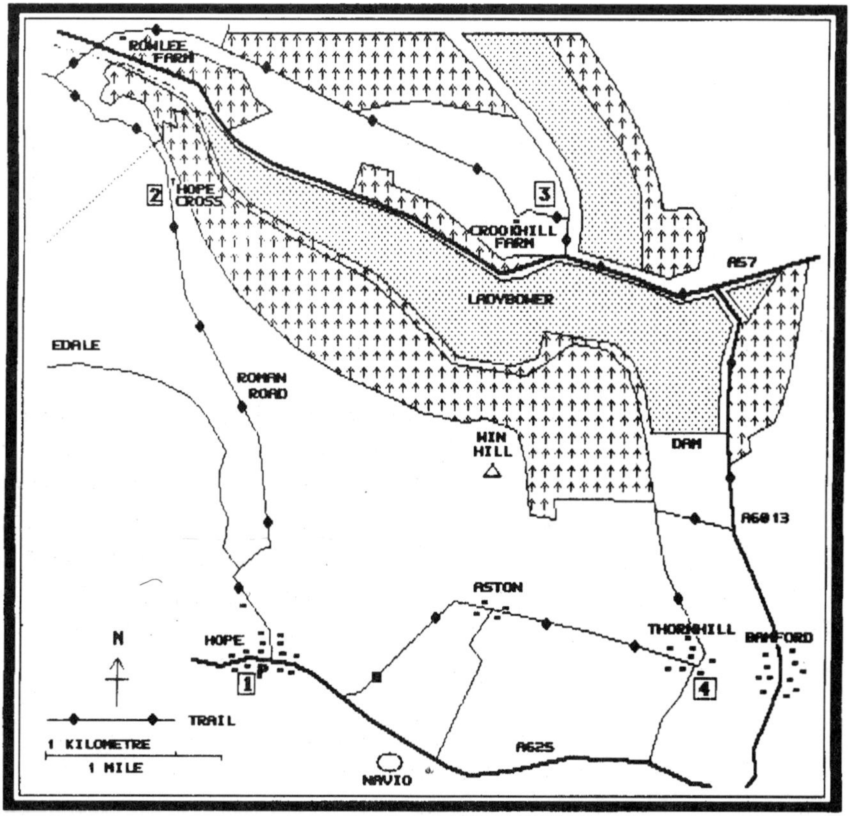

Win Hill is the distinctive conical shaped peak on the northern edge of the Hope Valley. The hill is surrounded by spectacular countryside and there are outstanding views from all sides. To the west is the tranquil Vale of Edale, starting point for the Penine Way. On the northern flank, is the massive Ladybower reservoir. To the east are the high gritstone edges and south is the verdant Hope valley running up to Castleton and Mam Tor.

This trail executes a complete circumnavigation of the hill using a Roman road, forest tracks and country lanes and provides views of great scenic beauty throughout its length.

POINT 1

Our starting point is Hope village, a km. or so east of Castleton on the A625. There is a car park in the centre of the village with a 'pay and display' arrangement.

POINT 1 TO POINT 2

From the village take the road leading north to Edale. Pass the Cheshire Cheese pub and continue under the railway line to a bridge over the river. Cross over the river and turn immediately right up a lane marked cul-de-sac. Follow the lane for two km. to a gate where the lane continues as a rough track. This track follows the route of a Roman road which once linked the fort of Navio to the east of Hope with settlements to the north. As the track climbs gently, magnificent views of the Vale Of Edale open up to your left. In the centre of the valley is the village of Edale, starting point for the Penine Way. To the north of Edale the hills rise to the bleak plateau of Kinder Scout, the highest mountain in the Peak District.

After approximately two kms. you will arrive at Hope Cross, a stone pillar surmounted by a square block carved with the directions of Hope, Edale, Glossop and Sheffield.

Win Hill from Ladybower

POINT 2 TO POINT 3

Pass through two gates to where a track crosses at right angles. Ignore this and carry straight on for a km. to Blackley Clough. Cross the stream, continue around the hillside and descend to meet a track. Turn right over the bridge and climb up to the A57.

Take the lane almost directly opposite and climb steeply for half a km. past Rowlee Farm. Follow the lane up the hill for a km. Where the lane bends left by the forest take the track to your right by a stone gate post. Turn left where the track divides. Continue along the edge of the forest, for just over a km. to where the track turns sharp left into the forest. Carry straight on a bridleway along the edge of the forest and climb for three kms. onto Crook Hill. The views over the Derwent Valley and Ladybower from this part of the trail are fantastic. From Crook Hill descend to Crook Hill Farm and follow the lane down to the road alongside Ladybower Reservoir.

POINT 3 TO POINT 4

Turn right and follow the road for a km. to the A57. Turn left over the arched concrete bridge and turn right after one and a half kms. onto the A6013 for Bamford. Follow the road for two kms. past the Ladybower dam and turn right onto a minor road across the base of the dam. At the far side of the dam turn left follow a minor road south for about four kms. to the village of Thornhill.

POINT 4 TO POINT 1

Turn right in the village on a road marked 'unsuitable for motors' and continue up the hill towards Aston. When you arrive at Aston carry straight on through the village and down Aston Lane.

Follow this lane for one and a half kms. to meet the A625. Turn right and follow the road back to the finishing point in Hope village.

TRAIL 4 - THE HIGH PEAK CIRCUIT

Distance: 50 kilometres (33 miles)

Terrain: Hilly, rough tracks, bridleways and minor roads.

Grading: Difficult.

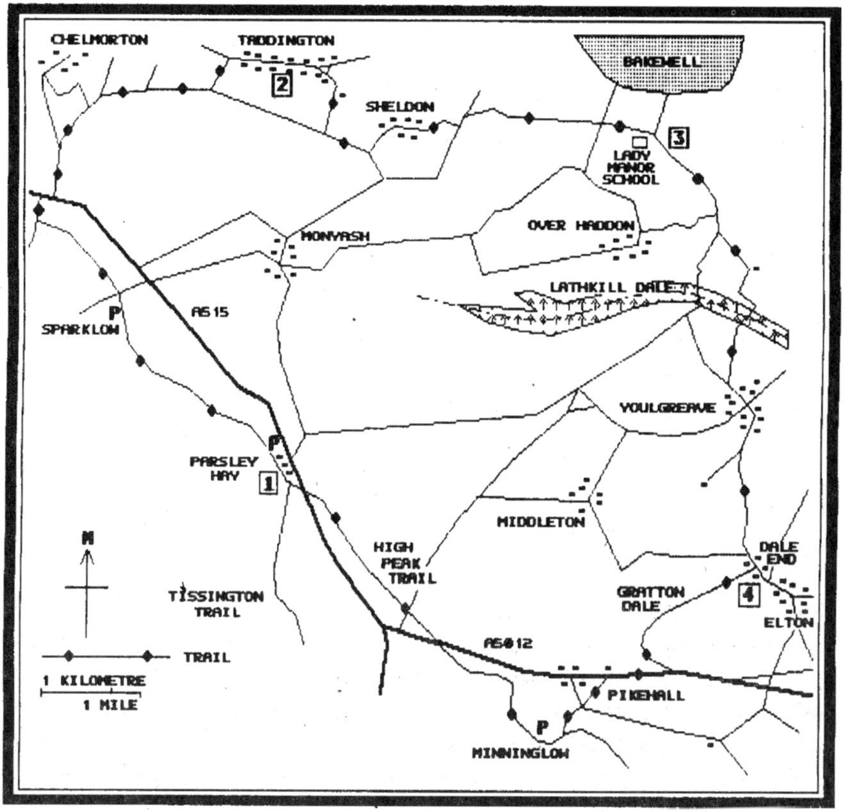

This route derives its name from the High Peak Trail, a long distance footpath/cycleway that follows the disused Cromford and High Peak railway line. The line linked the Peak Canal at Whaley Bridge with the Cromford Canal near Matlock and was unusual in that it included several inclines where the trains had to be hauled by static steam engines. It was opened in 1831 and sections of the track remained in use until 1967.

Following its closure, the track was acquired by Derbyshire County Council and the Peak District Planning Board and converted into a 25 km. path for walkers and cyclists. The High Peak Trail traverses some of the finest countryside in the National Park through gently rolling green hills covered with a lattice of white limestone dry stone walls. This circuit combines the northern half of the High Peak Trail with the picturesque villages of the surrounding area to make a superb long distance route.

POINT 1

Our starting point is Parsley Hay car park on the High Peak Trail. The car park is signposted on the west side of the A515 Buxton to Ashbourne road, fifteen kms. south east of Buxton.

POINT 1 TO POINT 2

From the car park head north along the High Peak Trail towards Buxton. After about four kms. the trail passes through a car park at Sparklow. Continue along the trail for a further three kms. to where the trail terminates at a lane facing a quarry. Turn left up the lane to the main road and then right along the main road for a short distance. Be careful, the traffic on this road is fast.

Turn left down the road towards Chelmorton and after a km. take the cart track leading off to your right. Follow the track for three kms. to a crossroads. Carry straight on, follow the road for three kms. and take a left hand fork to Taddington. The road climbs over a small hill and descends to the village.

POINT 2 TO POINT 3

Taddington is a sleepy little village with a long main street comprising stone cottages, a church and, of course, a pub. The village was not always so peaceful. Before the bypass was built it was on the main Buxton to Bakewell road.

Turn right down the main street and about one hundred metres after the Queens Arms the road forks. Take the right hand fork and follow the narrow lane over a hill for three kms. to Over Wheal Farm. At this point the road becomes a rough track that descends steeply to the head of Deepdale and then climbs to meet a minor road. Turn left along the road for a km. and then turn left for Sheldon.

Sheldon is another delightful Derbyshire village where time seems to have stood still. There is a bench outside the chapel where you can catch your breath and admire the surroundings.

Follow the road down through the village to a T-junction. Turn left and almost immediately right onto a lane. Follow this lane for about five kms. until you reach a crossroads above Bakewell. Carry straight on, passing Lady Manor school on your right, until you reach a T-junction.

POINT 3 TO POINT 4

Turn right and follow the road towards Youlgreave. After a km. you will pass Norton Barn Farm on your left and a further half km. brings you to a right hand bend marked by chevrons.

Packhorse Bridge Across The River Lathkill

Leave the road at this point, pass through a gate and follow a bridleway along the wall to a farm. Just before the farm turn right through a wooden gate and follow the fence to the bottom corner of the field. Turn left through the gate and follow the track down into the woods.

This section of track is steep and quite rough and you will probably need to dismount. At the bottom is Lathkill Dale and a picturesque stone packhorse bridge across the river. On one side of the bridge is a waterfall and on the other a large pool.

As you cross the bridge look down into the water and you will probably see the largest trout you have ever seen. The pool is full of these superb fish that are almost as numerous as the private fishing signs. Climb the lane at the other side of the bridge and turn left into Youlgreave.

Youlgreave, a once prosperous lead mining village, is now a popular tourist spot. In June the village is thronged with visitors for the well dressing ceremonies that take place at five local wells. The church, which dates back to the twelfth century, is one of the finest in the Peak District and has a most impressive spire. Of particular interest is the twelfth century font, which depicts a salamander lying on its back. This priceless object was discarded by the villagers of nearby Elton who have regretted it ever since. They later had a copy made for their own church. The seventeenth century Old Hall is also worthy of a visit.

When you have finished your exploration of the village, our route lies on the road to the right of the church. Follow this road towards the village of Elton.

POINT 4 TO POINT 1

After five kms. you will enter the hamlet of Dale End. Turn right through a wooden gate by the telephone box onto a bridleway that leads to Gratton Dale. One of the lesser known dales, Gratton is secluded and undisturbed. The dale is a haven for wildlife and you will be greeted by a cacophony of bird-song.

Follow the track into the dale, ignoring a track going off to your left over a bridge. As you enter the dale there is an old lime kiln on your right with a plaque showing how it was used. The track proceeds, flanked by limestone ridges, through this lush valley filled with hawthorn bushes and derelict limestone walls.

After three kms. you will emerge from the dale and cross the fields to the A5012. Turn right and after half a km. turn left into a minor road opposite Mouldridge Grange. Follow the road for a km. and turn right onto the High Peak Trail at the Minninglow car park.

Our route now proceeds along the High Peak Trail through ten kms. of splendid rolling limestone country back to the finishing point at Parsley Hay.

TRAIL 5 - GOYT VALLEY

Distance: 26 kilometres (16 miles)

Terrain: Hilly, rough tracks, bridleways, minor roads and a short stretch of main road.

Grading: Moderate.

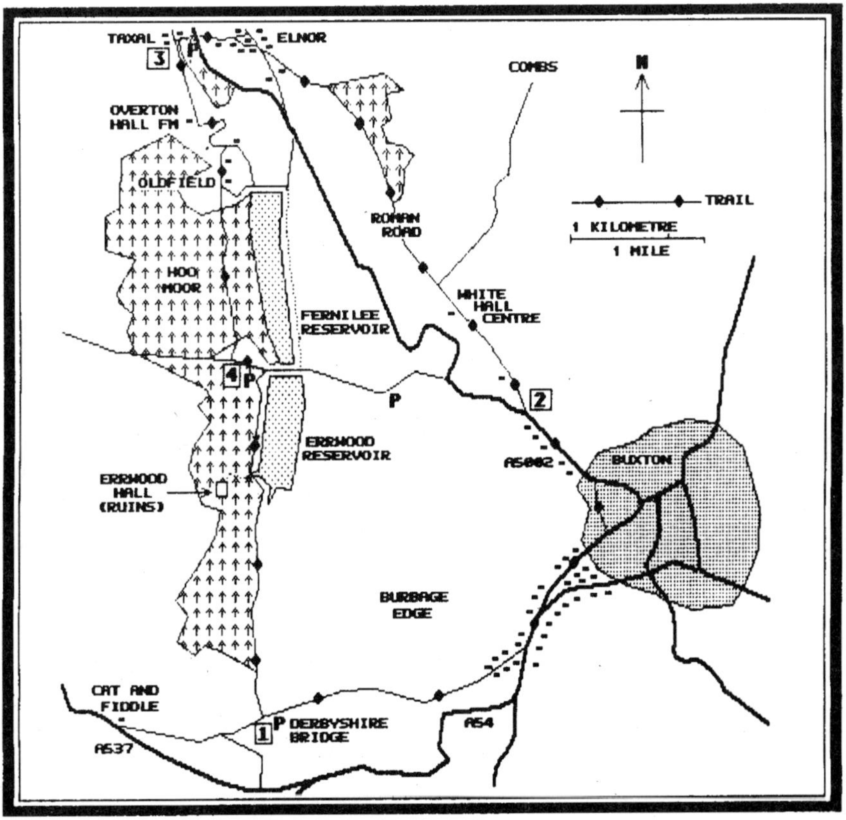

The Goyt Valley is an area of outstanding natural beauty between Buxton and Macclesfield. The valley contains two reservoirs that serve the nearby conurbation of Stockport and provides leisure facilities, including walking, sailing and cycling.

Originally flooded in 1938 to form the Fernilee reservoir, a second dam was built in 1967 for the Errwood reservoir and it is this dam that also carries the road across the valley. Prior to the flooding the valley was a farming community presided over by the Grimshaw family who owned the Errwood estate on the western side of the valley. The palatial Errwood Hall was built by Samuel Grimshaw in 1830 and was the centre for his flamboyant lifestyle. Grimshaw planted thousands of rhododendrons around the estate which still provide a blaze of colour in May each year. Regrettably, the Hall was abandoned in 1938 when the reservoir was built and now lies in ruins.

The scenic grandeur of the valley is undeniable. The wooded lower slopes of the valley merge into the purple heather of the moors above and make a stunning backdrop for the brightly coloured sails of the boats on Errwood reservoir. In summer months the road through the valley is closed to traffic on Sundays and large numbers of visitors wander through the valley to admire its beauty.

In order to incorporate the full length of this magnificent valley and to add further interest, the outward leg journeys via Buxton and follows the route of a Roman road to reach the far end. The trail then returns along the entire length of the Goyt Valley.

POINT 1

Our starting point is at Derbyshire Bridge car park two kms. east of the Cat and Fiddle Inn.

Turn north off the A537 Buxton to Macclesfield road by the junction with the A54. Follow the road down hill, turn right at the bottom and the car park is a few hundred metres further along the road.

POINT 1 TO POINT 2

Follow a rough track to the left of the car park up the hill and onto the moors. The track traverses a bleak stretch of moorland for two kms. before descending steeply. As you descend, the spa town of Buxton is revealed, nestling in the valley below. Continue downwards through a gate and between two rows of cottages to reach the main road.

Turn left along the road towards the town centre. If you wish to explore Buxton, continue into the centre and then when you are ready, take the A5004 Whaley Bridge road. There is much to see in this popular spa town. Besides some magnificent architecture, there is the Opera House, an award winning museum and art gallery, the Pavilion Gardens and a spa-water swimming pool.

If you do not wish to visit the town, continue along the road for a km..and turn left into Carlisle Road before you reach the centre. Follow the road for half a km. to a T-junction, turn left and then left again onto Manchester Road (A5004). Continue along the road for one and a half kms. to where it bends sharply to the left. On the opposite side of the road between the chevron signs there is a lane marked with a cul-de-sac sign.

POINT 2 TO POINT 3

Turn right onto this lane and follow it uphill for half a km. This is the route of a Roman road.

Pass through a gate onto a rough track, follow it over the edge of Combs Moss for two kms. and descend to White Hall Open Country Pursuits centre. As you descend the hill, there are spectacular views of Combs Valley to your right, with the reservoir glinting in the distance.

Continue along the lane, ignoring a right turn, and climb to the brow of a hill. From this point the Goyt Valley begins to come into view on your left. The lane now descends for five kms. to join a road at the village of Elnor. On the right by the junction are the remains of an ancient cross.

Turn right and then left into Shallcross Avenue through a housing estate. Turn left at the T-junction and follow a tree-lined lane. Bear right at Shallcross Hall Farm and follow the lane down to the A5004. Cross the main road into a lay-by on the opposite side and look for a track that starts in the middle. Follow the track downhill into a wooded dell and cross the River Goyt in the bottom. Climb the track on the other side that runs alongside St. James Church cemetery to reach the quiet hamlet of Taxal. You are now at the northern end of the Goyt Valley.

POINT 3 TO POINT 4

Turn left and follow the lane for two kms. to Overton Hall Farm. Turn left again and descend the hill into a wooded glade. Pass through a gate and climb the hill to Knipe Farm. Just before the farm turn right through a wooden gate onto a bridleway. The bridleway follows the edge of a wood for a short distance to a gate. Turn left through the gate and climb a walled track for a short distance to a gate by Normanwood Farm. Pass through the gate and follow a track for half a km. to Oldfield Farm. From this point Fernilee Reservoir begins to come into view in the valley below.

Pass through the farm yard and bear right onto a track leading into the forest on Hoo Moor. The track meanders through the forest, providing excellent views up the valley. After three kms. the track meets a road. Turn left down the road and you will arrive at the west side of the Errwood dam.

POINT 4 TO POINT 1

Follow the road around to your right along the western bank of the Errwood reservoir. After about a km. you will come to a bridge across an inlet. The inlet is covered by rhododendrons that are a riot of colour when they are in full bloom.

Access to Errwood Hall is on foot only so chain your bike to the railings on the bridge and follow the path on the right hand side of the inlet up through the woods to the ruins. At the top of the hill you emerge into a grassy dell populated by trees and rhododendrons. Cross a footbridge and climb a short distance to a ruined stone building. This was a coal mine that served the hall and local community. Together with farm produce from the valley, the hall must have been quite self sufficient.

The ruins of Errwood Hall are a short distance down the hillside. Built in 1830 by Samuel Grimshaw to Italian designs, the hall reflected the majestic lifestyle of its owner. The Grimshaws were renowned for entertaining lavishly and had an army of foreign servants. The hall, which by then was a shadow of its former glory, was demolished in 1938 when the Fernilee reservoir was built. It was believed that the presence of inhabitants in the valley would contaminate the water supply. Ironically, modern water treatment techniques allow the reservoirs to be used for fishing and sailing and the magnificent hall need not have been lost.

Above the hall on a wooded knoll is the family cemetery that has been thoughtfully restored by North West Water. One of the graves is the captain of Grimshaw's ocean going yacht, a further illustration of the family's considerable wealth.

Errwood Reservoir

A km. to the north is a small shrine erected in memory of a Spanish governess Delores de Bergrin who taught the Grimshaw children at the hall. The shrine is a circular stone building with a conical tiled roof, niche windows and low wooden door. Inside is a small altar that is often decorated by fresh flowers.

When you have completed your exploration of the ruins, retrace your route back down the hill to the road and turn right. Continuing along the road you enter a pleasant wooded glade as the road climbs steadily out of the valley. The road follows the route of the river Goyt that runs through the trees below. As you continue to climb, the aspect changes gradually from woodland to moorland. The hill seems interminable but the gradient is reasonable and the scenery dramatic. After six kms. of climbing from the valley floor, you will arrive back at Derbyshire Bridge and the finishing point of this trail.

TRAIL 6 - LADYBOWER

Distance: 22 kilometres (15 miles)

Terrain: Mostly level, rough tracks, bridleways and minor roads.

Grading: Moderate.

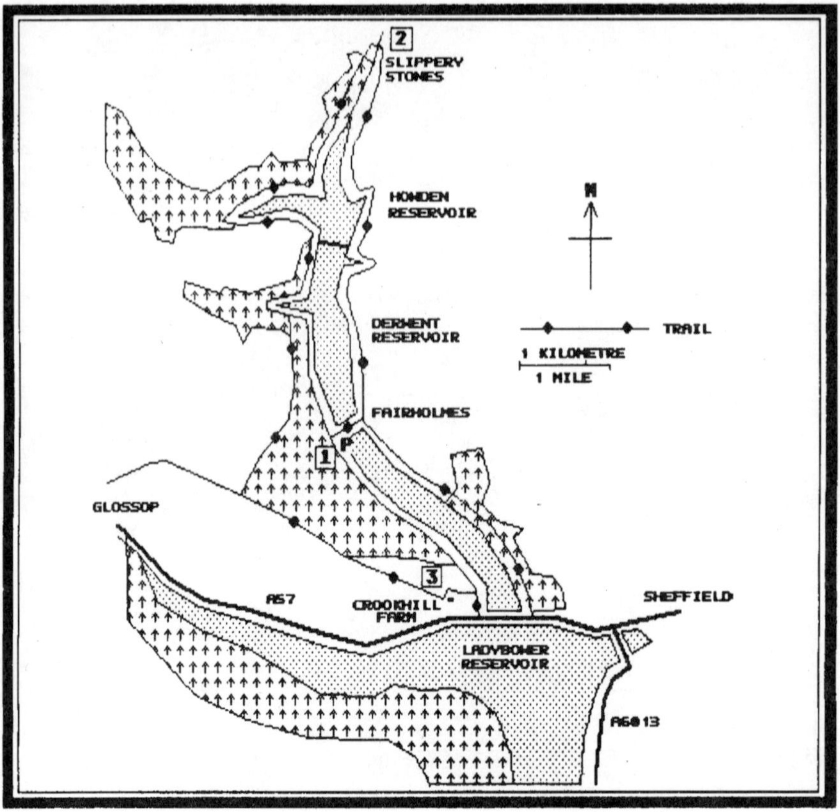

The Howden, Derwent and Ladybower reservoirs were built in 1902, 1916 and 1935 respectively and serve the cities of Derby, Nottingham and Leicester. Ladybower is the largest man made reservoir in England. The reservoirs were formed by flooding the picturesque Derwent Valley, sadly destroying the villages of Derwent and Ashopton in the process. The ruins of the villages can still be seen during periods of drought.

Constructed of huge blocks of sandstone with turreted walls, the Howden and Derwent dams are most impressive structures. Their similarity to the dams in the industrial heartland of Germany led to the area being used for training the famous Dambusters Squadron during the second world war.

Barnes Wallis's bouncing bomb was tested at Ladybower before being used to such devastating effect in Germany. On the 17th May 1943 Wing Commander Guy Gibson and his 617 Squadron carried out a raid on the Eder and Mohne dams, successfully breaching both. Walls of water were unleashed down the Eder and Ruhr valleys causing chaos and wrecking much of Germany's armaments industry. The raid was later acknowledged to have made a substantial contribution to the allied war effort. The Derwent Valley was later used as the backdrop for the Dambusters film made after the war.

This trail completes a circuit of the magnificent Derwent Valley, encompassing all three reservoirs. The area around Ladybower is extremely popular and you should avoid this trail at bank holiday weekends.

POINT 1

The trail starts from the car park at Fairholmes between the Ladybower and Derwent reservoirs.

Turn north off the A57 Glossop to Sheffield road on the west side of the Ladybower bridge. The car park is on your right approximately five kms. down this road.

POINT 1 TO POINT 2

From the car, park head east across the base of the Derwent dam. Follow the track up to your right and then turn left along the eastern bank of the Derwent reservoir. The track climbs steadily to the Howden dam where there are magnificent views of the reservoir and surrounding hills.

From the dam, the track follows the bank of the Howden reservoir to a narrow tip, where the river Derwent feeds in. The track now runs along the edge of a wood with the river Derwent below in the trees. After a km. or so you will see a bridge below at a place called Slippery Stones.

POINT 2 TO POINT 3

Drop down the path, cross the bridge and turn left into the woods. After about half a km. the track emerges from the trees and joins a road. This road is closed to traffic at weekends except for a mini-bus which ferries walkers back and forth.

Follow the road along the west bank of the reservoir. After a km. you will reach an inlet where the road makes a long detour. At the other side of the detour you will arrive at the Howden dam and can see this huge stone structure at close quarters. Two kms. further, brings you to a second smaller inlet. Just after the hairpin bend at the end of the inlet watch out for a bridleway leading into the forest to your right. Follow this track up through the trees and climb steadily alongside Nabs Wood. Cross the brow of the hill and descend to Lockerbrook Farm and Outdoor Activity Centre.

The Derwent Dam

After approximately half a km. the track bends around to the right. Follow a track leading off to your left by a stone gate post and bear left where the track divides. The track runs alongside the woods for a km. Where the track turns left into the forest follow the bridleway that carries straight on.

The bridleway continues for three kms. over the hill and descends to Crookhill Farm. This section again offers panoramic views of the surrounding area. Continue your descent for half a km. to reach the road. Turn right and follow the road for half a km. to the A57.

POINT 3 TO POINT 1

Ladybower reservoir is an inverted 'T' shape with an elegant arched concrete bridge that carries the A57 across its base. Turn left and cross this bridge and turn left again at the far side onto a bridleway. Don't be put off by the "private road" signs - these apply to a private driveway that has the same access road.

Pass through a gate onto the track that follows the eastern bank of the reservoir. As you follow the track, yet another aspect of this scenic valley is disclosed. After approximately five kms. the track joins a metalled road that leads back to Fairholmes and the finish of this trail.

TRAIL 7 - THE TISSINGTON CIRCUIT

Distance: 36 kilometres (24 miles)

Terrain: Hilly in parts, disused railway line, minor roads and bridleway.

Grading: Moderate.

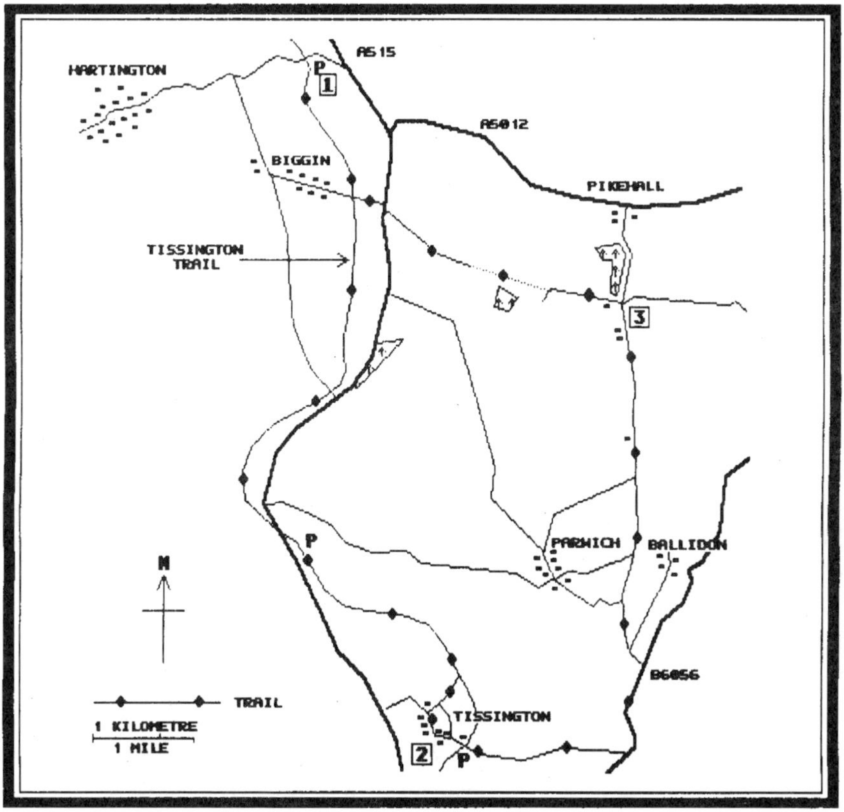

The outward leg of this trail uses the Tissington Trail, a disused railway line between Ashbourne and Buxton. Built by the London & North Western Railway Company in 1899 it carried limestone from the local quarries, farm produce and passengers but was never a great commercial success. The line was closed in 1967 and converted by the Peak Planning Board and Derbyshire County Council, to their everlasting credit, into a leisure trail for walking, cycling and horse riding. The Trail runs from Parsley Hay in the north, where it joins the High Peak Trail, to Mapleton Lane near Ashbourne. Having visited the enchanting village of Tissington, our route returns via the country lanes and tracks around Parwich.

POINT 1

Our starting point is the car park on the Tissington Trail at the old Hartington Station. Turn west off the A515 Buxton to Ashbourne road onto the B5054 for Hartington. The entrance to the car park is on the left just before the railway viaduct. A nominal parking fee is levied that you are requested to deposit in an 'honesty box'.

POINT 1 TO POINT 2

Join the Trail by the signal box that has been carefully preserved and now serves as a tourist information centre in summer months. Note the cast iron boundary posts that bear the initials of the London & North Western Railway Company. Turn left along the trail and follow it into the beautiful rolling limestone country of the southern Peak District. Apart from a few cuttings there are largely uninterrupted views of the surrounding scenery. After ten kms. the Trail passes under the A515 to reach a car park near Alsop en le Dale.

Continue for a further two kms. and the Trail bends to the left and passes under a stone bridge and through a cutting. A second bridge leads to Cake Low Cutting that has been designated as a nature reserve. The third bridge after the car park is our exit from the Trail. Ignore the makeshift steps on your right as you pass under the bridge and continue for a further fifty metres to where a sloping path leads over a stile to the top of the bridge. Turn left down the tree lined lane for half a km. into Tissington village. As you enter the village bear right at the junction and drop down to the main street.

In my estimation Tissington is the loveliest village in the Peak District. The layout is spacious with broad grass verges and open areas. There is seventeenth century hall, a Norman church, a duck pond and no less than five wells, namely: Hall, Hands, Coffin, Town and Yew Tree. The village is thronged with visitors on Ascension Day in May when all five wells are dressed with floral tableaux. Across the road under a lean-to roof is a rough map of the village showing the position of each well. It is well worth (excuse the pun) touring around the village to examine each well in turn.

Turn left down the main street and on the right you will immediately see the sinister architecture of Tissington Hall. This impressive building would make an ideal setting for a Dracula film. Built in 1609 the Hall has been home to the Fitzherbert family ever since. In the eighteenth century, Maria Fitzherbert married the Prince of Wales(later King George IV)but the marriage was later dissolved when George's father withheld his consent because of the Fitzherbert's Roman Catholic faith.

Opposite the entrance is Hall Well covered by an ornate limestone canopy. From the well a steam flows into a cobbled channel that runs alongside the main street.

Further down on the left, raised from the street on a grassy mound, is the superb Norman church. This remarkably well preserved example of Norman architecture was built in the twelfth century and has, amongst many points of interest, an unusual carved stone font.

Tissington Hall

At the end of the street is the old School House, now converted into a tea room and to the left of this is the duck pond. Follow the road around to your left and the road divides. To continue your tour, take the left fork that completes a circle around the village. Our route out of the village follows the right fork.

POINT 2 TO POINT 3

The road out of the village passes the entrance to the Tissington Trail car park and crosses a bridge over the trail to emerge in open countryside. An unfenced road continues for two kms. and descends to a ford across a stream. In the dry season you can cross the ford without getting your feet wet but in wet weather I would recommend that you use the wooden bridge provided. Turn left at the junction with the B6056 and follow the road for one and a half kms. to a left turn for Ballidon and Parwich.

Turn left through an avenue of trees and continue along the road, ignoring a right hand turn to Ballidon, for two kms. to a junction. The left turn leads to Parwich but our route lies straight ahead on the road to Pikehall. The road climbs steeply now for one and a half kms. On your right you can just see the top of the spoil heaps of the huge Ballidon quarry that is fortunately concealed from view.

Shortly before the brow of the hill a road joins from the left and from the top there are commanding views of the surrounding area. Drop down the other side of the hill and a second road joins from the left. Continue along the road for two kms., climbing steadily to a crossroads by the start of a wood on the left hand side of the road.

POINT 3 TO POINT 1

Turn left and follow the lane past a bungalow. Head towards a stand of trees on the horizon. After a km. the lane bends sharply to the right and there are two metal gates facing you. Take the left hand gate and follow the bridleway alongside the wall to a gate at the top left hand corner of the field. Continue along this track across the top of the hill passing through two further gates. The prospect from the top of the hill is extensive, covering most of the southern half of the National Park.

The track descends to the A515 and almost directly opposite is the turning for Biggin village. Follow this minor road for half a km. and you will see the Tissington Trail crossing the road over a bridge. Take the track to your right just before the bridge and rejoin the Trail heading northwards. Two kms. of easy cycling brings you back to Hartington Station and the end of this trail.

TRAIL 8 - THREE SHIRE HEADS AND LUD'S CHURCH

Distance: 27 kilometres (18 miles)

Terrain: Hilly, minor roads, rough tracks and a short section of main road.

Grading: Moderate.

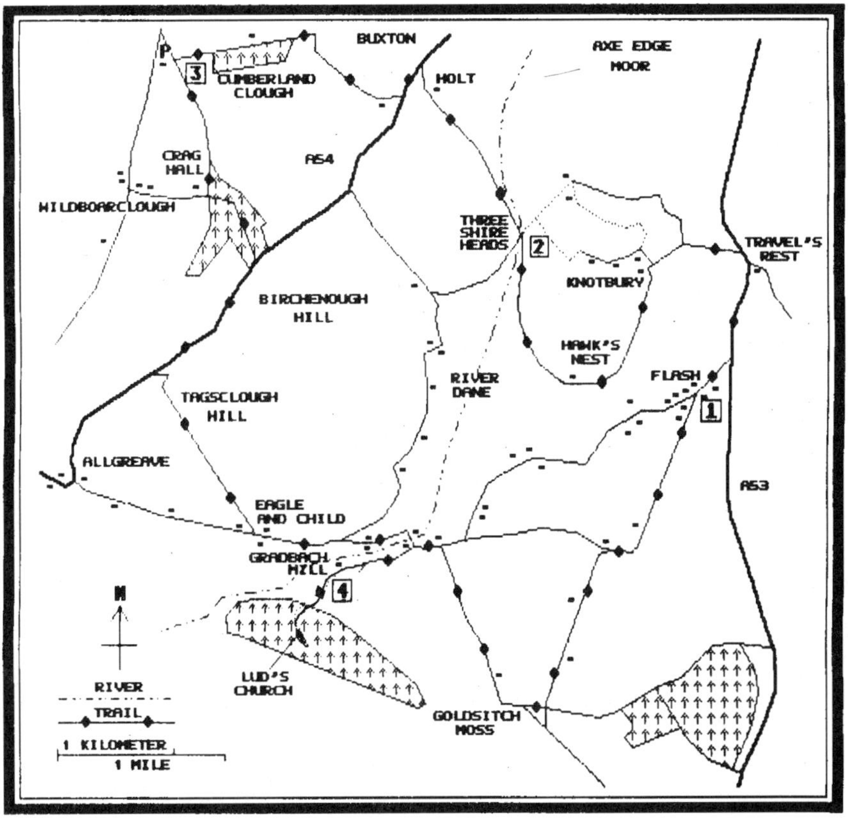

The river Dane rises on Axe Edge Moor above Buxton and meanders down through the western Peak District onto the Cheshire Plain, where it joins the river Weaver. Three Shire Heads is an enchanting spot where two streams merge to form the Dane. There are two stone packhorse bridges, a waterfall and large pool beneath. As its name implies, it is the boundary between three counties - Derbyshire, Cheshire and Staffordshire. The place is steeped in history is now a popular destination for walkers and bikers.

Lud's Church - sometimes known as Lud's Cave - is a deep narrow gorge in the woods above Gradbach. The entrances are well concealed and the gorge has been used as a hideout by outlaws and religious groups through the ages. The place derives its name from Walter de Ludank the leader of a persecuted religious sect called the Lollards whose meetings were held in the gorge.

POINT 1

Our starting point is Flash, the highest village in England. Turn west off the A53 Buxton to Leek road half a km. south of the Travellers Rest Inn. Flash is half a km. along this road. There are a few car parking spaces in the village centre or you may be able to use the car park outside the village hall that is on your left as you enter the village. If there is no space in the village, use the car park at Gradbach and start from point 4.

POINT 1 TO POINT 2

Before you set out take some time to explore the village. A neat collection of stone built buildings it boasts the highest post office and village pub (the New Inn) in England. I can recommend the hospitality in the latter that makes an excellent stop for refreshments after you have completed the trail.

Further along the main street on the opposite side to the New Inn is a large building with a double flight of stone steps. This was the Methodist Chapel built in 1784 and visited by the founder of the Methodist faith, John Wesley. At the other end of the village there is also a sturdy stone built church. The village is reputed to have been the origin of the word 'flash' meaning gaudy or showy. The word was derived from 'Flash money' produced by forgers who frequented the area.

From Flash head out of the village back towards the Buxton road. Turn left at the main road, follow it for half a km. past the Travellers Rest and then take a minor road on your left to Knotbury. Follow the road down the valley for two kms. passing three roads coming in from your right.

Just after the third junction the road bends sharp left. Continue along the road for a further two kms. bearing right under a group of rocks called Hawk's Nest. Bear right again onto a rough track by Turn Edge Farm. This track leads for two kms. down a delightful bracken covered valley beside the river Dane to Three Shire Heads.

In addition to its undoubted beauty the place has a notorious reputation. Until the late nineteenth century it was used as a refuge by rogues and scoundrels because the authorities were restricted to operating within their county limits. Outlaws would simply move across the boundary to evade arrest. These unsavoury characters also attracted a number of barbarous 'sports' to the location including cock fighting and bare knuckle boxing.

Take some time out to admire the views of the waterfall and bridges. As you stand on the main bridge facing down stream, to your left is Staffordshire, to the right is Cheshire and behind you is Derbyshire.

POINT 2 TO POINT 3

Cross the main bridge and turn right. Follow a bridleway alongside the river Dane for half a km. and climb up the hill past Holt Farm to reach the A54.

Three Shire Heads

Turn left along the road and after a few hundred metres turn right onto a track marked "unsuitable for vehicles". Take care on this busy stretch of road. Pass through the gate, follow the track over the hill for one and a half kms. and descend to Cumberland Clough.

This is a picturesque spot, set against the backdrop of Shutlingsloe, where Cumberland Brook tumbles over a waterfall and disappears into a copse of conifers. Turn left and descend the clough for just over a km., crossing the Cumberland Brook to meet the road by Clough House. On your left is a car park and picnic area.

POINT 3 TO POINT 4

Our route is to the right. Follow the road for just over a km. to Crag Hall. This impressive stone building is the country seat of Lord Derby. Bear left at the junction shortly after the hall and follow a road, lined by trees and rhododendrons, uphill for half a km. to reach the A54.

Turn right, follow the road for a km. and take a track, marked unsuitable for vehicles, on your left through a gate. Follow the track up the hill and bear left where the track divides. Continue along this track over Tagsclough Hill for two kms., pausing to admire the excellent views from the brow of the hill. On the other side of the hill the track meets a road. The building on your right at this point was formerly the Eagle and Child Inn.

Turn left and follow the road for just over a km. to a bridge over the river Dane. Climb up the hill on the other side of the bridge for a few hundred metres and turn right by a farm towards the youth hostel. Follow this lane for a km, passing a car park on your right, to where it divides. Take the right hand fork and drop down the hill to take a look at Gradbach Mill. This splendid stone building with arched georgian windows was formerly a silk mill powered by the waters of the river Dane, which runs alongside. Recently restored, the mill is now a youth hostel providing low cost accommodation for young people exploring the National Park.

After your visit to the Mill, return up the hill to where the lane divides by two stone gate posts and turn right up the hill.

Ignore the left hand turn at the brow of the hill and follow the lane down to your right into the hamlet of Gradbach. Carry straight on and the lane becomes a rough track. Bear right as you approach a wooden gate and descend the hill to the river. Cross the river by the stepping stones, turn right and follow the bridleway which climbs up through the woods to your left. Follow the broad track up through the trees for half a km. to where it meets a footpath.

You can only reach Lud's Church on foot so chain your bike to a tree and follow the footpath to your left. After about two hundred metres there is a group of rocks on your right with a gap in the centre. This is the entrance to Lud's Church. If you examine the rocks on the left hand side you will see the word 'LUD' carved in the stone with an arrow pointing into the gorge. Pass through the entrance and climb down the steps into the gorge.

A more inhospitable place is difficult to imagine. Less than five metres wide with a mud floor, the moss covered rock walls tower 20 metres on each side, making the gorge dark and dank. Legend has it that the gorge was used by Robin Hood and his followers to escape the clutches of the Sheriff of Nottingham. Even in the height of summer the air is cold and there is always an eerie atmosphere in this secluded refuge.

When you have completed your exploration, retrace your route back to Gradbach.

POINT 4 TO POINT 1

Follow the lane from Gradbach back to the road. Turn right and after a short distance turn right again over a stone bridge towards Royal Cottage and Leek. Continue on this road for two kms. to the junction at Goldsitch Moss.

On the way you will pass the rather grand sounding Royal Cottage, which is a small stone house on your left. From Goldsitch Moss the forbidding Eastern flank of the Roaches looms large to your right. This large expanse of moorland is inhabited by wallabies which escaped from the grounds of nearby Swythamley Hall during the Second World War. Surprisingly, these marsupials survived our harsh climate and a small wild colony was established. Many a visitor to the area has wondered about his sanity after seeing one of these creatures bounding across the heather. If you are fortunate enough to see the wallabies be careful not to disturb them.

Follow the road around sharp left and bear left again at the next junction towards Flash. Follow this road for two kms. to a T-junction. Turn right up the hill and follow the road for two kms. to the hillside village of Flash and the finish of this trail.

TRAIL 9 - THE MATLOCK CIRCUIT

Distance: 36 kilometres (24 miles)

Terrain: Hilly, minor roads, rough tracks, disused railway line and canal towpath.

Grading: Moderate.

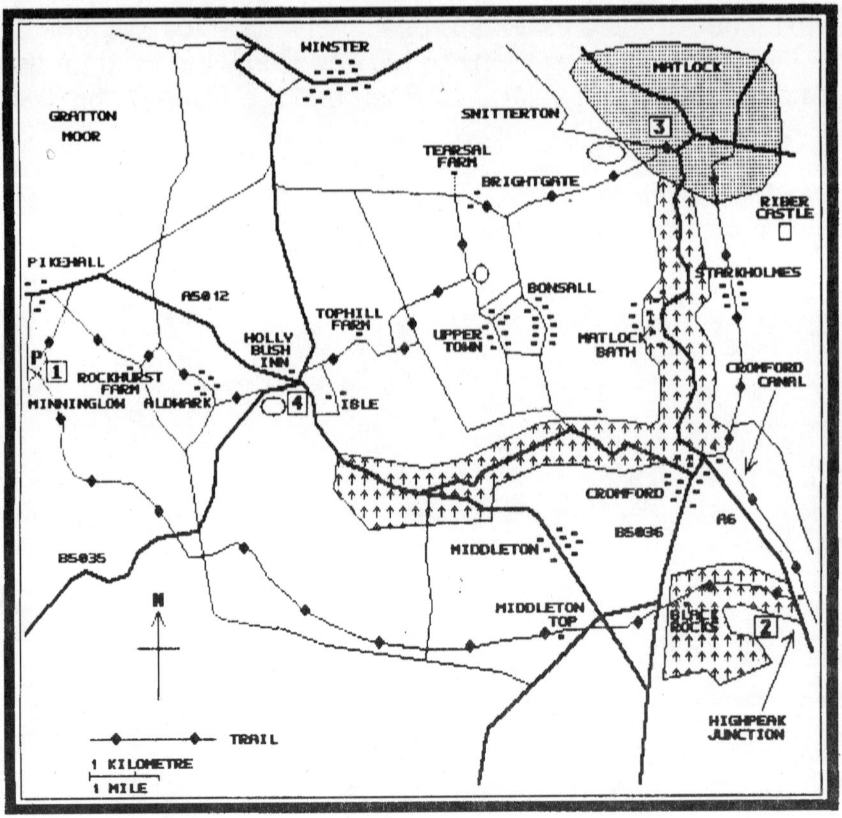

Situated at the head of a deep limestone gorge on the banks of the river Derwent, Matlock is a bustling town on the south east fringe of the National Park. The original Matlock, a small village surrounding St. Giles church, expanded rapidly at the end of the seventeenth century when it became the intersection of five turnpikes. Together with nearby Matlock Bath, the town became a popular tourist resort during the eighteenth century and remains so to this day.

Further down the gorge, thermal springs were discovered at the end of the seventeenth century. Numerous baths and hotels grew up around the springs to establish the spa resort of Matlock Bath. During the eighteenth century Matlock Bath was immensely popular with the wealthy and genteel and had some of the finest hotels in the country. In 1853 an enterprising local mill owner, John Smedley, opened a hydro (hotel and baths) at Matlock Bank. The hydro was a great success and was extended several times. Its proprietor used the profits from the hydro to build Ribber Castle on the hill above the gorge, from which he could look down on his empire. With the coming of the railway in 1849 the spa became more accessible to the masses and by the end of the century most of the well-heeled had moved away.

Today's Matlock Bath has all the trappings of a modern tourist resort including an amusement park, slot machine arcades and a cable car ride. Its founders would no doubt strongly disapprove.

Downstream from Matlock Bath is the village of Cromford where Sir Richard Arkwright established the world's first cotton spinning factory in 1769 that is now an industrial museum. In 1793 the Cromford Canal was opened further enhancing the area's importance as a communications hub. Designed by William Jessop, the canal was fourteen and a half miles long and connected to the Erwash Canal at Langley Mill. In 1814 a further canal project was approved by Parliament, linking the Cromford Canal with the Peak Forest Canal at Whaley Bridge.

The purpose of the canal was to provide a trade route between south Lancashire and Derbyshire. Design work was started but the engineering difficulties of running a canal across the porous limestone terrain proved to be insurmountable and the canal was abandoned in favour of a railway.

The 33 mile link was built by Josiah Jessop (son of the canal builder) and completed in 1831. The influence of canal design can be seen in the rail link construction. Instead of the gradual gradients used on most railways it features a series of steep inclines, similar to the flights of locks found on canals. These are connected by long level sections. There are a total of nine inclines, eight of which had static steam engines to haul the trains. One of the engine houses has been carefully preserved as a museum at Middleton Top.

Initially, the trains were horse drawn along the level sections until locomotives were introduced in 1840. Goods were transferred from barges to railway trucks at High Peak Junction near Cromford. The workshops here have also been turned into an industrial museum. A passenger service was introduced in 1850 but was discontinued in 1877 after an accident in which a passenger was killed. The 33 mile journey took 24 hours to complete.

The northern section of the line was closed in 1892 but parts of the southern half continued to operate until 1967. The line was then acquired by Derbyshire County Council and the Peak Planning Board who converted it into the High Peak Trail, a track for walkers and cyclists.

The forethought of these authorities has provided a beautiful and undisturbed route across the limestone country of the southern Peak District. The trail covers twenty four kms. from High Peak Junction to Downlow near Buxton.

The High Peak Trail

This trail attempts to capture some of the history and scenic beauty of this fascinating area. The route utilises the southern section of the High Peak Trail, a stretch of the Cromford Canal and returns via the lead mining country to the north of Matlock. There is much to see on this trail and you should allocate a full day if you intend to visit all the points of interest.

POINT 1

Our starting point is a car park on the High Peak Trail at Minninglow. Turn south off the A5012 at Pikehall and follow the narrow lane for a km. The car park is just under a railway bridge on your left.

POINT 1 TO POINT 2

Leave the car park by the south entrance onto the High Peak Trail. The track progresses through gently undulating green hills criss-crossed by dry stone walls. Its construction is an amazing feat of civil engineering with deep cuttings through limestone hills and embankments supported by carefully crafted stone buttresses.

After twelve kms. you will reach the first of the inclines at Hopton. This incline was the only one of the nine to be worked by the locomotives and at 1 in 14 was easily the steepest in the country. Descend the incline and continue through the tunnel for a km. to the visitors centre at Middleton Top. The engine house at Middleton Top has been preserved as a museum. It is open to the public at weekends and is well worth a visit. The museum contains the original steam winding engine that hauled trains up the 1 in 8 Middleton incline via a continuous cable system.

One of eight supplied by Butterley Company in 1829, the two cylinder beam engine worked continuously until its closure in 1967.

There is a railway truck at the top of the incline, showing how the trains were attached to the cable via chains. At the bottom of the incline the lower pulley wheel can seen on the right hand side of the track. Continue along the trail for two kms. to Black Rocks. The massive rocks towering above the track are a popular haunt for climbers.

There are also picnic areas, guided walks through the forest and magnificent views of the Matlock gorge. The empty shell of the engine house lies beside the track at the top of Pasture Incline. At 1320 yards this is the longest of the inclines and has a gradient of 1 in 8.

Towards the bottom a 'catch pit' was installed following an accident in 1888 when two runaway trucks left the track at High Peak Junction, clearing the canal and main line railway before coming to rest in a field.

At the bottom of the hill, the trail passes under the main road to arrive at High Peak Junction and the Cromford Canal. The collection of buildings were workshops where the railway rolling stock was maintained. Now a museum, the workshops give a fascinating insight into the heavy engineering techniques of a bygone era.

POINT 2 TO POINT 3

From the museum cross the wooden bridge and turn left along the canal towpath. Cyclists are permitted on the towpath provided that they **give precedence to pedestrians**. Follow the towpath for three kms. alongside the railway and river Derwent to Cromford Wharf. Turn left and after half a km. you will arrive at Arkwright's Mill. The mill has been converted into an industrial museum and is well worth a visit. When you have finished exploring, you have a choice of routes.

You can continue past the mill and turn right onto the A6 through the Matlock gorge. Although there is much to see on this route the road is extremely busy and you may wish to consider the following quieter alternative.

Retrace your route to the wharf. Continue along the road, cross a bridge over the river Derwent and turn left up the hill to Starkholmes. As you climb the hill there are spectacular views of the gorge and the cable cars that span its reach from the Heights Of Abraham. The road climbs steadily for three kms. to the village of Starkholmes.

The impressive profile of John Smedley's Ribber Castle now comes into view on the skyline above. Smedley died in 1874 and the castle fell into decay. Its ruins are now occupied by a wildlife park that is yet another place worth visiting. The access road goes off to your right. From Starkholmes, descend the hill for two kms., passing St. Giles church on your left, to arrive at the junction with the A615.

POINT 3 TO POINT 4

Turn left along the road into Matlock passing the riverside gardens on your left. Bear left at the roundabout over the river bridge and carry straight on at the crossroads on the other side. Follow the road right towards Snitterton and after half a km. take a left turn onto a narrow lane to Masson. The lane climbs unrelentingly for two kms. and continues along the top for a further two kms. to a T-junction. Turn right and follow the road to Brightgate. Turn left onto a rough track opposite the entrance to Tearsall Farm. Follow the track for two kms., bearing right by a quarry.

Turn left when you reach the road and then right onto a cart track after a km. Spoil heaps and machinery in the fields beside the road provide evidence of the lead mining activity that dominated this area. Follow the track across the hill top for a km. and carry straight on at the crossroads towards Tophill Farm. Farmers are not noted for their tidiness but Tophill is a scrap dealer's dream. There are discarded vehicles, engines and farm machinery everywhere. Drop down the hill, picking your way through the junk to arrive at the rear of the Hollybush Inn.

POINT 4 TO POINT 1

Turn left and carry straight on at the junction with the main road. Just before the quarry entrance take a lane on your right to Aldwark. Climb the hill for one and a half kms. and turn right into the hamlet. Aldwark is a sleepy place typical of so many hamlets in the Peak District. It is good to see that many of the derelict stone buildings are now being carefully restored.

Follow the road through the hamlet for two kms. to a road junction. Turn left up the hill for a km. and turn right onto a farm track by Rockhurst Farm. The track adjacent to the farm is often deep in liquid manure as I once discovered to my cost. If you stick close to the right hand wall you can avoid this fragrant concoction. The track soon improves and crosses three kms. of delightful open countryside to meet a metalled road. Turn left and a km. brings you to the car park at Minninglow and the finish of this trail.

TRAIL 10 - THE UPPER DOVE VALLEY

Distance: 24 kilometres (16 miles)

Terrain: Hilly, rough tracks, disused railway line and minor roads.

Grading: Moderate.

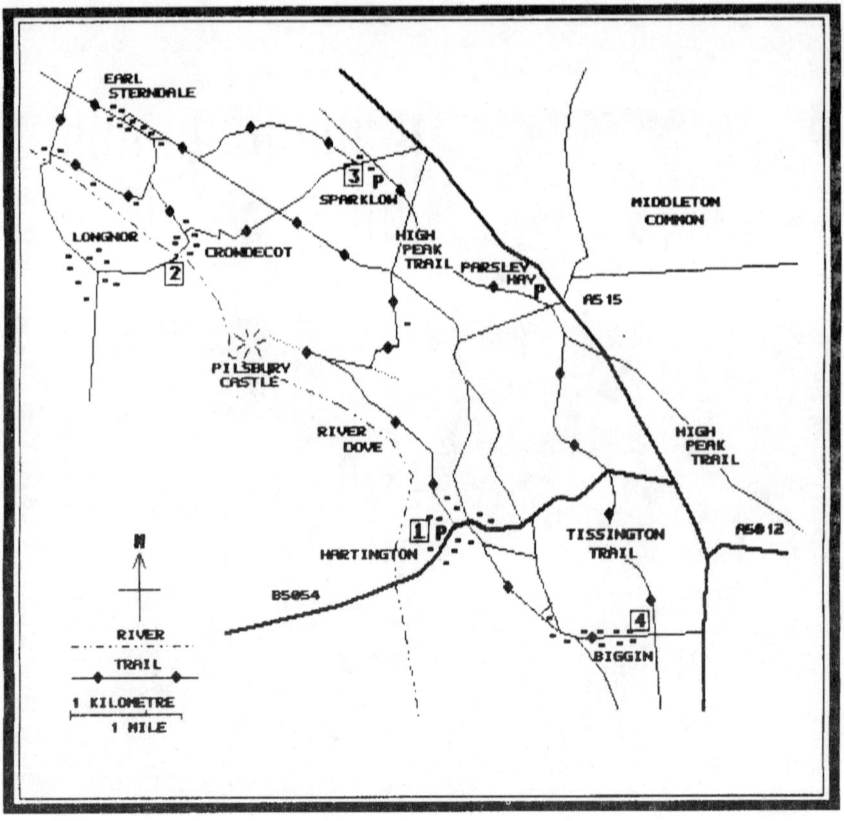

The lower part of the Dove Valley (Dovedale) is probably the most popular area in the Peak District but alas is closed to cyclists. The upper reaches of the river Dove however, are equally picturesque and fortunately more accessible to mountain bikes.

This trail starts from the bustling village of Hartington in the heart of the Peak District. With its elegant stone buildings and duck pond, the village is full of olde worlde charm. On a summer's day, its gift shops and cafes are thronged with visitors.

Hartington produces some of the finest Stilton cheese in the country. You can buy samples of this delicacy in a tiny shop by the duck pond. The thirteenth century church is also well worth a visit. Set back on a hillside on the east side of the village the church contains many interesting artifacts.

POINT 1

Hartington is situated about eighteen kms. southeast of Buxton. Turn west off the A515 onto the B5054, the village is about four kms. along this road. Park in the centre by the duck pond or in the 'pay and display' car park on the west side of the village.

POINT 1 TO POINT 2

Assuming that you have parked in the car park, ride into the village centre and turn left past the duck pond. Head north out of the village following a lane along the Dove valley. The splendour of the valley soon becomes apparent. A lush green carpet stretches towards the distant Hollins and Chrome hills at the head of the valley. Continue along the lane, passing through several gates. After about four kms. the lane turns sharply right and is signposted for Longnor.

Leave the lane at this point and follow a track down to your left. After half a km. you will arrive at a mound with a limestone outcrop. This is all that remains of Pilsbury Castle, a Norman Fort built by William the Conqueror in 1068 to quell local unrest.

Upper Dove Valley

Pilsbury is a fine example of the motte and bailey construction. A plaque on the wall shows an illustration of the castle as it was in its original state and gives some of the historical details.

Retrace your route back to the lane and bear left up the hill. The lane climbs steadily for three kms. to meet a crossroads. Turn left at the crossroads along the road towards Earl Sterndale. Follow the road for a further two kms. to another crossroads, turn left for Crowdecote and descend sharply for one and a half kms. to the village. As you descend stunning views of the Upper Dove Valley are revealed before you.

POINT 2 TO POINT 3

Turn right down a minor road just before the Pack Horse Inn. Follow this road for just over a km. and turn left onto a track by a house. Follow the track through a farm yard and along the tranquil valley floor for two kms. to meet the road at Glutton Bridge. Turn right and climb the hill for a km. to a crossroads. Turn right into the sleepy hillside village of Earl Sterndale. Continue through the village passing the Quiet Woman Inn on your right. The ladies amongst you will no doubt be offended at it's blatantly sexist sign that depicts a headless woman.

On the south side of the village turn left for Pilsbury/Hartington and continue along the road for two kms. to where an unmarked track goes off to your left. Turn left and follow the track over the hill and down into the next valley. After about three kms. you will come to a T-junction with the Royal Oak pub on your left. Turn left and cross over the road to a lane going off to your right that drops down the hill and joins the High Peak Trail at Sparklow car park.

POINT 3 TO POINT 4

Turn right along the High Peak Trail and follow it for about four kms. to Parsley Hay. Shortly after Parsley Hay follow the Tissington Trail to your right.

After about three kms. you will pass the signal box at what used to be Hartington station. Carry on for a further three kms. to where the trail crosses a road at the village of Biggin. Leave the trail at this point and turn right down the road into the centre of the village.

POINT 4 TO POINT 1

Follow the road down through the village to a T- junction. Turn right and after about twenty five metres take a lane to your left between two houses. The house on the right has a set of stone steps at the side.

The lane climbs steeply and is joined by other lanes coming in from both sides. Ignore these and carry on straight up the hill. The summit provides panoramic views of Beresford Dale, Wolfscote Dale and the Manifold Valley. Nestling in the valley below is your destination - Hartington. A short decent brings you to a road. Turn left and the road leads to the centre of the village and the end of this trail.

TRAIL 11 - MAM TOR AND EDALE

Distance: 33 kilometres (22 miles)

Terrain: Very hilly, bridleways and minor roads.
Note: This trail covers long stretches of grass and should be avoided in wet weather.

Grading: Difficult.

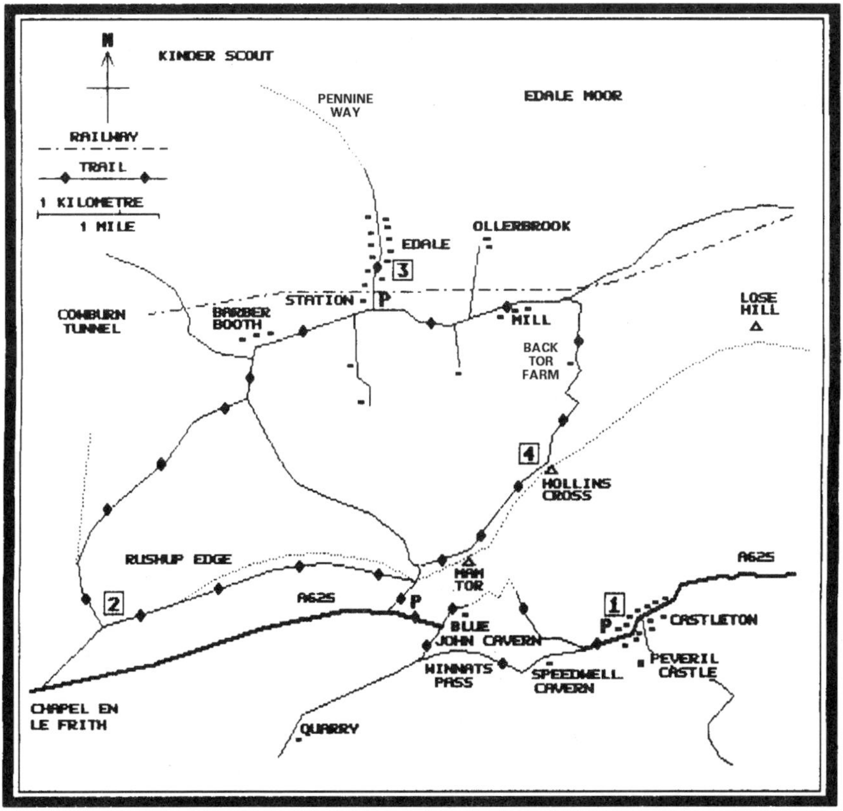

This trail combines the spectacular and fascinating mountain of Mam Tor with the picturesque countryside around the Vale Of Edale.

Mam Tor, known locally as the 'Shimmering Mountain' is famous for its massive land slip that took away one side of the mountain including the road below. The land slip, believed to be 3000 years old, moves regularly, usually when a long dry spell is followed by heavy rain.

Ignoring its reputation, the Manchester and Sheffield Turnpike Company built a road across the land slip in 1802. A more gradual alternative to the nearby Winnats Pass, the road was very popular with the farmers and merchants of the day. However, the land slip continued its inexorable progress and the road was continuously under repair. Following the long hot summer of 1976 the road deteriorated rapidly and was finally closed in 1979 after two-metre gaps appeared in the road's surface.

POINT 1

Our starting point is the charming village of Castleton on the A625 to the west of Sheffield. There are a few parking spaces in the centre or a 'pay and display' car park on the west side of the village.

Castleton is inundated with souvenir shops selling semi-precious stones from the surrounding caverns. In summer months and at weekends the village is overwhelmed with visitors. Overlooking the village is Peveril Castle that dates back to Norman times and from which the village presumably got its name. There are also numerous caverns, where, for a modest fee, you can spend a few fascinating hours exploring the underworld.

POINT 1 TO POINT 2

Head westwards out of Castleton and bear right at the junction for Winnats Pass. Carry on past the Treak Cliff Cavern where the road is closed to vehicles.

The Land Slip - Mam Tor

The road across the land slip is still negotiable with care so continue through the gate and up the hill. You will soon encounter spectacular evidence of the force of Mother Nature.

Huge sections of the carriageway have been twisted and broken as if it were a strip of liquorice. At the points where the road is severed, you can see multiple layers of tarmacadum from the continuous repair programme. In places, the surface is over a metre thick. If you look up you will see the cause of the problem. One side of Mam Tor is totally displaced leaving a huge crater on the side of the mountain.

Negotiate your way across the land slip until you reach a gate. Continue up the road to a junction, passing Blue John Cavern on your left. Turn right along the road for just under a km. and then right again for Edale by a car park. Follow the road up through the trees and just before the brow of the hill turn left through a wooden gate onto a bridleway. Climb up for half a km. onto Rushup Edge.

There is a footpath along the edge but this is out of bounds to cyclists. The bridleway runs a few metres lower down the hillside through a wooden gate. Follow the bridleway, which, compared with the footpath, is little more than a sheep track, along Rushup Edge. The views to your left are extensive, stretching over the moors to Chapel - en - le - Frith in the distance. After three kms. you will reach a wooden gate where the bridleway merges with the footpath. Turn left through the gate and follow the track downhill for a km. to the junction of three tracks by a cairn and green sign.

POINT 2 TO POINT 3

Turn right and follow the bridleway along a plateau for half a km. At this point the massive bulk of Kinder Scout fills the skyline ahead of you. Kinder Scout is the highest mountain in the Peak District and covers a huge area. It's summit is a vast moorland plateau etched by deep gullies.

Many people lose their way on this forbidding mountain. There are no less than nine aircraft wrecks on and around the mountain. These were mostly bombers from the second world war, which came to grief whilst returning to nearby Manchester.

Follow the track around to the right and begin to descend into Edale. The valley is like a vast green bowl with the village of Edale nestling in the middle. Trains ply back and forth along the Manchester to Sheffield line, disappearing into the Cowburn Tunnel just below to your left. The track is rough and has been made worse by off-road vehicles. Negotiate your way carefully down the hillside for three kms. to meet a road. Turn left and drop down the hill to Barber Booth. Cross the bridge and bear right along the valley for two kms. to Edale station.

POINT 3 TO POINT 4

Turn left under the railway line into Edale. The village is a collection of fine stone buildings scattered along a lane. There is a sturdy stone church and on your left and a little further along the Old Nags Head, which is the official starting point of the Pennine Way. The village acts like a magnet to walkers and bikers and is always busy.

When you have finished exploring the village return under the railway line to the valley road. Turn left and continue along the road for two kms. Shortly after passing an old mill on your right and just before the railway bridge, turn right into a lane towards Back Tor Farm. Follow the lane uphill for a km, passing through two wooden gates. After the second wooden gate bear right on a bridleway heading up the hill. The next km. is a steep climb to the summit of Hollins Cross.

As you climb, yet another aspect of the Vale Of Edale is revealed. The summit of Hollins Cross is marked by a memorial to Tom Hyett, a late member of Long Eaton Ramblers. The views from Hollins Cross are simply superb. To the south the magnificent Hope Valley stretches into the distance. If you look below to your right you will get a birds-eye view of the Mam Tor land slip that you negotiated earlier.The only blot on an otherwise unblemished landscape is Hope Valley cement works.

Although the works undoubtedly provides much needed employment for the area, its conspicuous siting, ugly construction and smoke plume detract from one of the finest views in the Peak District.

POINT 4 TO POINT 1

Turn right and follow the ridge towards Mam Tor. After a km. the footpath and bridleway part company and the bridleway runs in parallel, to the right of the path. As you approach the summit, the bridleway bends around to the right, following the line of a wooden fence. If you wish to climb to the summit, chain your bike to the fence at this point and follow the footpath to the top. The views from the top are equal to, if not better than, those from Hollins Cross and well worth the short climb. Mam Tor was once the site of hill-top fort, the ramparts of which can still be seen surrounding the summit.

Return to your bike and follow the bridleway for half a km. to meet the road. Turn left, climb over the hill and descend to the A625. Turn left along the road for half a km. and right at the next junction. Climb for half a km. and turn left for Castleton and Winnats Pass.

The next three kms. descend steeply through a deep gorge with limestone crags towering on either side. This is Winnats Pass. Towards the bottom of the hill you will pass Speedwell Cavern where boat tours are organised through the underground caves. A short distance further and you reach the continuation of the A625. Turn right and follow the road for half a km. back to Castleton and the finish of this trail.

TRAIL 12 - THE MANIFOLD CIRCUIT

Distance: 33 kilometres (22 miles)

Terrain: Hilly, minor roads and disused railway track.

Grading: Easy.

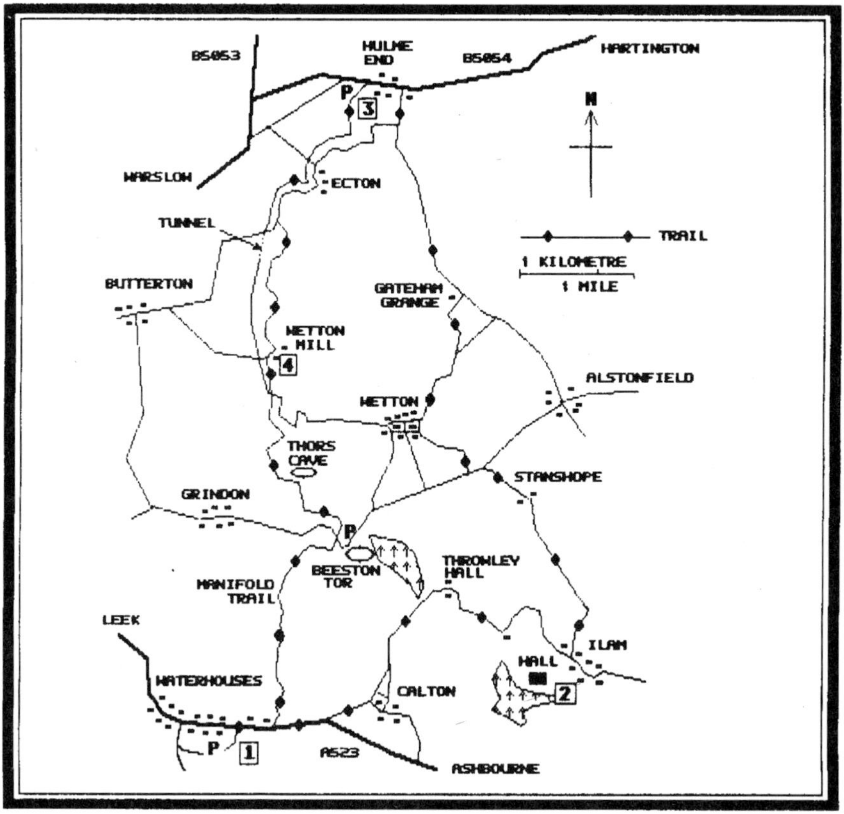

The river Manifold rises near Longnor and runs south for twenty two kms. to join the river Dove at Ilam. The lower half of its course runs through the fascinating Manifold valley. A thickly wooded steep-sided limestone gorge, the valley is a haven for birds and other wildlife. The valley also has many places of interest including the magnificent Thors Cave. During summer months and dry spells the river mysteriously flows underground from Wetton Mill and reappears at Ilam, leaving what appears to be a dried up river bed.

Ecton, at the northern end of the valley, was the centre of a thriving copper mining industry from the seventeenth to the nineteenth century. The mines were owned by the Duke of Devonshire and profits from the enterprise were used to improve Chatsworth and build some of the splendid buildings in Buxton.

Ore from the mines was initially transported along the valley by packhorse to the smelters in the Churnet Valley near Leek. The packhorse trail was later replaced by the Leek and Manifold Light Railway that ran from Hulme End, at the top end of the valley, through Waterhouses to Leek. The railway was closed in 1934 and later converted into the Manifold Trail, a long distance track for cyclists and walkers. The Trail runs fifteen kms. from Hulme End to Waterhouses and forms the return leg of our journey.

POINT 1

Our start point is the car park at Waterhouses. Turn south to Cauldon off the A583 Leek to Ashbourne road in the centre of the village by the public house. Pass under the railway bridge and turn immediately left into the car park. The car park is on the site of the former Waterhouses station. One of the original buildings is now used by a cycle hire business.

POINT 1 TO POINT 2

Leave the car park at the opposite end to the entrance and drop down under a railway bridge to the main road. Turn right along the main road, passing the Manifold Trail on your left. Climb up the hill for half a km. and take a left turn to Calton. Climb the hill to the village and turn left for Ilam/Throwley. Bear left at the next two junctions and follow the road for two kms. to Throwley Hall. Turn right through the farm yard and follow the track down the hill towards Ilam.

As you descend the hill, you will get your first sight of the river Manifold, or at least the dry river bed, which runs along the valley below. Cross over a stone bridge at the bottom of the hill and a further km. brings you to the village of Ilam. Note the collection of old farm machinery on your left as you enter the village.

Ilam is a delightful estate village that is very popular with tourists during summer months. The church dates back to Saxon times and was restored in 1618. In the church yard are two Viking crosses that are dated approximately 900 AD. The cottages are built in an unusual Alpine style that adds to the charm and fascination of the village. In the centre there is a Gothic cross erected in 1840 as a memorial to Mrs. Watts Russell of Ilam Hall. The Hall is an impressive stone building set in spacious grounds by a loop in the river. It was rebuilt in 1828 and acquired by the National Trust in 1934. The Hall is now used as a Youth Hostel and outdoor pursuits centre. The Hall was also used as the location Catherine Cookson's "The Mallens" TV series.

POINT 2 TO POINT 3

From the village, retrace your route on the Throwley road to the collection of old farm machinery.

Turn right up the hill for Wetton and Alstonfield. The road climbs steadily for about three kms. to the village of Stanshope. Follow the road left and right through the village and down the hill to a junction at Hopedale. Turn left up the hill towards Wetton, following the road around to the left and then right. On the edge of Wetton take a lane to your right and continue along to the next junction.

Turn right and follow the road for approximately two kms., ignoring a turning to your right, to a junction at Gateham Grange. Turn left towards Hulme End and descend the hill for about three kms. to the main road by the Manifold Hotel. Turn left along the main road for a few hundred metres and then left into the Manifold Trail car park.

POINT 3 TO POINT 4

Join the Trail at the far end of the car park and follow the river Manifold. After about three kms. the Trail joins the road by a tunnel. To your right is Ecton that was a centre of copper mining activity. Very little remains of this other than the overgrown spoil heaps and some of the miner's cottages.

Turn left along the road, cross the river bridge and turn immediately right through a metal gate. The next three kms. are absolutely delightful. The Trail follows a track, lined with hawthorn bushes, through fields alongside the river. On your left you will see one of the disused mine shafts(these are dangerous and should not be entered). Bear left where the track divides and shortly after this point you will see a splendid circular stone dovecote on the opposite bank. After three kms. you will reach a farm. Turn right and drop down a short hill to reach Wetton Mill.

This is an excellent spot for a well earned rest. A small cafe serves ice-cream in the summer and hot soup in the winter. You can sit amidst the limestone buildings by the banks of the river and watch the world go by.

Wetton Mill

POINT 4 TO POINT 1

From Wetton Mill, cross the stone bridge and turn left. At this point, two roads run in parallel for just under a km. (it doesn't matter which one you take).

Where the roads rejoin you will see the Manifold Trail continuing south across a wooden bridge, Follow the Trail for half a km. and towering above you to the left is the gaping mouth of Thors Cave. The huge entrance is unmistakeable, measuring ten metres by seven and giving the cave a commanding vantage point over the valley and surrounding countryside. Archaeologists have discovered animal bones and stone implements that suggest the cave was occupied from the Bronze Age onwards.

Leave your bike by the footbridge and make the short climb to the cave. You will not be disappointed. Not only is the cave impressive but the views of the valley are magnificent.

Return to the Trail and continue southwards. Two kms. further along on your left is Beeston Tor, an 80 metre limestone buttress that provides excellent rock climbing. The Trail leaves the Manifold Valley at this point. Take the right hand track as you cross the road and the Trail sweeps around to the right. The remaining six kms. of the Trail follow the river Hamps through an enchanting wooded dale back to Waterhouses.

Turn right along the main road for half a km. and the left under the railway bridge to the car park and finish of this trail.

If you are in need of refreshments after the ride I can recommend the Yew Tree at nearby Cauldon. The pub was built in the fifthteenth century and has changed very little since. Winner of numerous awards, the Yew Tree is packed with antiquities and items of interest and is an experience in itself.

TRAIL 13 - AXE EDGE MOOR

Distance: 21 kilometres (14 miles)

Terrain: Hilly, moorland tracks, minor roads and a short stretch of main road.

Grading: Moderate.

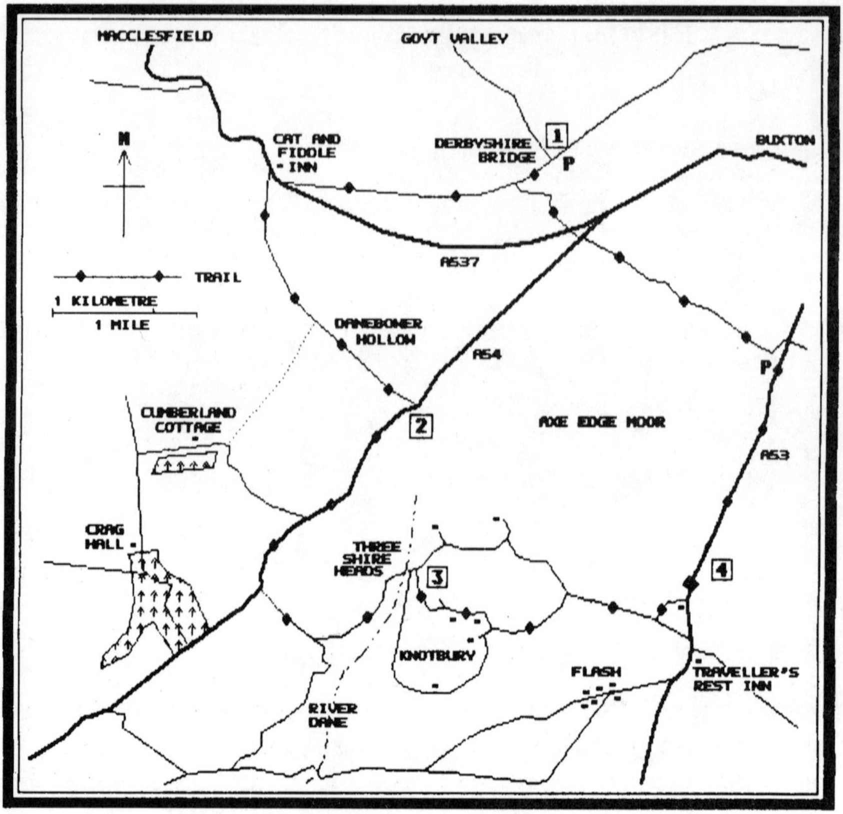

Axe Edge is a huge expanse of moorland to the west of Buxton. This high plateau forms a desolate landscape that has a strange almost haunting beauty. The peat surface absorbs water like a sponge and is a watershed which spawns many of the best known rivers in the Peak District. The Dove, Manifold and Wye run east to join the Trent and eventually the North Sea, whereas the Dane and Goyt find their way west to the Mersey and the Irish Sea.

In addition to its water resource, Axe Edge provided coal for local communities during the eighteenth and nineteenth centuries. Disused mine shafts and workings are scattered across the moor. This bleak raft of heather and bilberry conceals the secluded beauty spot of Three Shire Heads that is visited on this trail.

POINT 1

Our starting point is the car park at Derbyshire Bridge. Turn north off the A537 Buxton to Macclesfield road adjacent to the junction with the A54 three kms. east of the Cat And Fiddle Inn. Turn right at the bottom of the hill and the car park is two hundred metres further along the road.

POINT 1 TO POINT 2

From the car park head west towards the Cat And Fiddle Inn. The Cat And Fiddle is unmistakeable, occupying one of the highest points on the moor in splendid isolation. It is just eleven metres short of being the highest pub in England, second only to Tan Hill in the north Pennines. Join the main road and turn left onto a track directly opposite the pub. Follow this track for two kms. across open moorland. The aspect to the west is breathtaking with panoramic views across to the Cheshire Plain.

The pyramid shaped peak dominating the skyline is Shutlingsloe that towers above Wildboarclough valley. After a km. you will pass a path to Cumberland Brook going off to your right. Continue straight on for one and a half kms. to meet the A54.

POINT 2 TO POINT 3

Turn right along the road for about half a km. to an 'S' bend marked by chevrons. As you exit the bend take the lane going off to your left. Follow this lane along and down for about a km. and turn left onto a rough track marked for Three Shire Heads. The track leads down a delightful bracken-lined valley alongside the river to the remote beauty spot.

Three Shire Heads is an enchanting place where two streams merge to form the Dane. There are two stone packhorse bridges, a waterfall and large pool beneath. As its name implies, it is the boundary between the three counties of Derbyshire, Cheshire and Staffordshire. Until the end of the nineteenth century, the place was a haunt for rogues and vagabonds who used the borders to escape the clutches of the county authorities.

POINT 3 TO POINT 4

Turn right over the bridge and through the metal gate opposite. Carry your bike across a rough section of track and after two hundred metres, turn right over a bridge and through a wooden gate onto a bridleway leading to Knotbury. Climb up a rough track for half a km. to meet a lane. Turn right, follow the lane for half a km. and descend to a T-junction. Turn left and follow the road uphill. Take the second turning on your left and continue upwards for half a km. past a timber yard.

Follow the lane over the brow of the hill and descend to the A53.

Axe Edge Moor In Winter

POINT 4 TO POINT 1

Turn left along the A53 for two kms. On the right you can see where the gritstone landscape of Axe Edge merges with the limestone country to the east.

Just after a car park on your left, take a left turn back onto the moor. Climb the road and traverse across the moor for three kms. This is one of the highest points on the moor and there are superb views in all directions. The stark landscape has a dramatic beauty.

Descend to meet the A54, turn left and then right onto a narrow road that meets the A537. Cross the A537 and follow the road downhill for a km. Turn right and follow the road for a short distance back to Derbyshire Bridge and the finish of this trail.

TRAIL 14 - THE ROACHES FROM DANEBRIDGE

Distance: 33 kilometres (22 miles)

Terrain: Hilly, minor roads and bridleway.

Grading: Moderate.

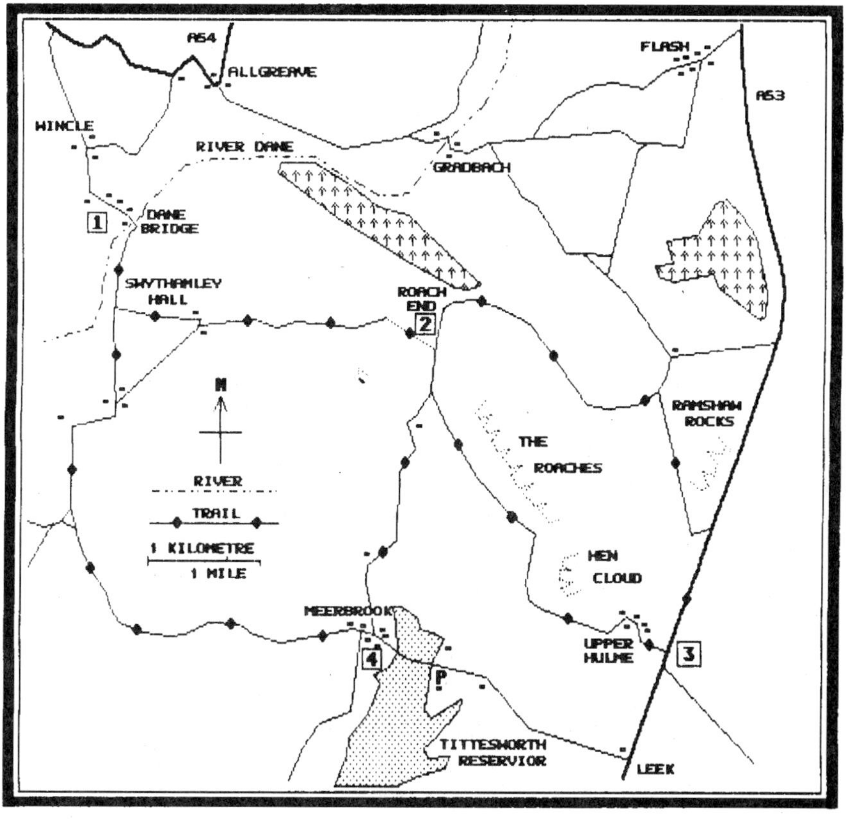

The Roaches runs for some six kms. and is one of the finest ridges in the Peak District. Formed from the red gritstone, which runs down the western edge of the National Park, the ridge provides excellent rock climbing and spectacular views of the surrounding area.

The southern point of the Roaches is an isolated rocky outcrop called Hen Cloud. The main ridge then runs northwards, starting with the rocks of Five Clouds and continuing from Roach End across the moors to the river Dane.

This trail completes a circuit of the Roaches, taking in the 'Best Kept Village' of Meerbrook and the picturesque Tittesworth reservoir. The scenery throughout the length of this trail is some of the best in the Peak District.

POINT 1

Our starting point is a popular beauty spot - Danebridge at Wincle. Take the road south to Wincle off A54 Buxton to Congleton road. Follow the road down through the village passing the Ship Inn on your left. At the bottom of the hill you will see Danebridge. Park on the left side of the road.

POINT 1 TO POINT 2

Follow the road across the bridge leading towards Meerbrook. The road climbs up the hill to a junction. Take the road to your left which skirts the grounds of Swithamley Hall. Shortly after passing a restored chapel on your left the road bends sharply to the right. Immediately after the bend turn left through a farm yard. Follow the lane upwards for two kms., noting the magnificent views to your right. The rocky ridge is the Roaches and nestling in the valley below is the village of Meerbrook and Tittesworth reservoir.

At the top of the lane you will arrive at a gate marked 'private'. Do not despair, take the bridleway to your right through a gate and follow the wall until you meet a minor road. Turn left and follow the road to another gate. You are now at Roach End.

POINT 2 TO POINT 3

Continue up the road and then descend across the back of the Roaches for three kms. The forbidding eastern flank of the Roaches looms large to your right and on your left the vast expanse of moorland is Goldsitch Moss. Ignore the limestone track going off to your right and take the next turning on your right. Follow the road for two kms. to meet the A53 by Ramshaw Rocks. Turn right down the road for just over a km. and turn right for Upper Hulme.

POINT 3 TO POINT 4

Follow the road down through the village bearing left through the factory yard. The road now climbs steeply revealing the full grandeur of the Roaches to your right. Levelling off, the road traverses the entire length of Hen Cloud and the Five Clouds giving a superb prospect of this rocky escarpment. The views below to your left are equally as stunning with the water of Tittesworth Reservoir glinting like a sheet of bright metal amidst a sea of green pasture.

Shortly after you have passed Hen Cloud there is a gate on your right where a footpath leads up onto the Roaches. If you are keen to do a spot of exploring, I suggest that you leave your bike here and ascend on foot. As you climb up to the ridge you will pass the 'hermits cave' that was occupied by a man and his wife until they were moved by the local authority in 1988.

The 'cave' is a simple stone structure built into the rock face. They obviously valued their privacy greatly. A sign with the blunt message 'trespassers will be shot' can still be seen on the wall outside. The man, known locally as the 'Lord Of The Roaches' is still seen on market days in nearby Leek. When asked what he would miss most from his life on the Roaches he said "the sunsets". If you are there in the late evening you will know exactly what he means.

The crags above are usually crowded with rock climbers. Many top climbers have learned their craft on these rugged slabs of gritstone. I understand that there are plans to turn the hermits cave into a refuge for climbers.

Returning to your bike, continue north along the side of the Roaches for almost three kms. and turn left towards Meerbrook. Follow the road downhill along pleasant lanes for four kms. to the village.

Meerbrook is an idyllic place and has won numerous awards for being the 'Best Kept Village' in Staffordshire. The road brings you out between the youth hostel and Lazy Trout Inn. Bear left and follow the road along for half a km. to where the bridge crosses Tittesworth Reservoir. The bridge provides an excellent vantage point from which to observe the reservoir and surrounding countryside.

The small stretch of water north of the bridge has a bird hide where the ornithologists amongst you can watch a wide variety of wading birds in peace and seclusion. Access to the hide is gained via a gate to your left on the other side of the bridge. On your right is a large car park and visitors centre run by Severn Trent Water. The centre features an adventure playground, natural history exhibition and cafe. I can thoroughly recommend the home made cakes served in the latter. As you can imagine the place is extremely popular in the summer.

"Hermit's Cave" — The Roaches

POINT 4 TO POINT 1

Return to Meerbrook and follow the road through the centre of the village towards Wincle.

After passing the village hall, the road begins to climb steeply and continues unrelentingly for over a km. Your effort is well rewarded, however, because the views from the top are breathtaking. The distinctive wedge shape of Bosley Cloud dominates the scene ahead and leads your eye through a gap to the Cheshire Plain beyond.

The road skirts the edge of a heather and bilberry moor, continues along a plateau and descends for two kms. to a junction. Carry straight on for Wincle and descend for a further km. to the hamlet of Gun End where the road bends sharply left and then right. Continue straight on at the next hairpin bend and drop down a narrow lane into a wooded glade. Climbing steeply up the other side, the lane meets a road from the right by the entrance to Swythamley Hall. Carry straight on for almost a km. to Danebridge and the finish of this trail.

TRAIL 15 - MACCLESFIELD FOREST AND WILDBOARCLOUGH

Distance: 21 kilometres (14 miles)

Terrain: Hilly, minor roads and rough tracks.

Grading: Moderate

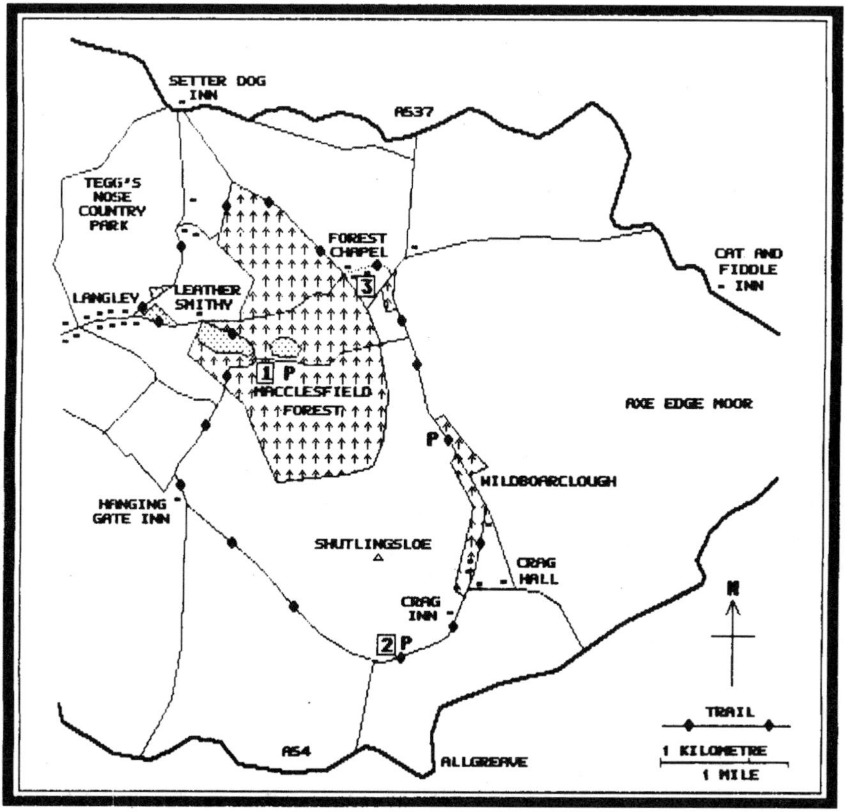

Macclesfield Forest dates back to medieval times when it covered a vast area from Stockport in the north to Congleton in the south. Now greatly reduced in area and with the deciduous trees replaced by conifers, the forest is still one of the largest areas of woodland in the Peak District and covers the hills to the East of Macclesfield like a vast green carpet.

The forest is home to an abundance of wildlife including a herd of Red Deer and a wide variety of birds and wildfowl. In addition to the leisure amenity and natural habitat, the forest provides water for the local community from the Ridgegate and Tentabank reservoirs and also a valuable timber crop.

To the east of the Forest is Wildboarclough one of the prettiest valleys in the Peak District. Sheltering between Axe Edge moor and the mighty bulk of Shutlingsloe the valley is a secluded paradise. Our route follows the road along the valley which intertwines with Clough Brook as it progresses through leafy glades and fertile meadows.

POINT 1

The starting point for this trail is the car park opposite Trentabank reservoir. Turn South off the A537 Macclesfield to Buxton road for Tegg's Nose country park by the Setter Dog Inn. Follow the road over the hill, past the entrance to the park, down the hill and turn left for Langley. From Langley turn left and after a km. turn right by the Leather Smithy Inn. Follow the road around the Ridgegate reservoir, bear left at the next junction and the car park is on the right opposite Trentabank reservoir.

Before you start on the trail take a few minutes to absorb the beauty of Trentabank reservoir.

Cross the road and follow a short track through the trees to the waters edge. The reservoir is surrounded by wooded hills and makes a delightful setting. You will invariably see a heron and numerous species of wildfowl.

POINT 1 TO POINT 2

Retrace your route back towards the car park, turn right down the hill for a few hundred metres and then left for Higher Sutton. The road climbs steeply initially and then gradually for two kms. To your right are extensive views over the Cheshire Plain and directly ahead is the prominent telecommunications tower on Croker Hill. Bear left at the next road junction and turn left again just after you pass the Hanging Gate Inn on your right.

Follow the road up the hill for one and a half kms. The prominent peak to your left is Shutlingsloe. Its distinctive pyramid shape makes it instantly recognisable from many distant points. Near the brow of the hill is an ancient stone pillar with a cross carved on each side. On the other side of the hill you descend for one and a half kms., ignoring the left turn to Higher Nabbs Farm and continuing down through Lower Nabbs Farm. Bear left at the road junction onto the Wildboarclough road.

POINT 2 TO POINT 3

As you head north along the road it soon becomes apparent why Wildboarclough is so popular. Clough Brook runs alongside the road tumbling over waterfalls as it gushes down the valley. There are lay-bys and seats by the side of the brook that are thronged with visitors in the summer. After just over a km. you will pass the Crag Inn on your left and approach the centre of the village. The bridge on your right bears a plaque commemorating the recent flood disaster.

Its substantial walls were swept away by the weight of water. The valley suffered a major catastrophe when it was hit by a flash flood on the 24th May 1989. A pipe carrying the brook through an embankment at the top of the valley became blocked and the water from a cloud burst quickly accumulated to form a huge lake. The embankment broke under the weight of water and unleashed a tidal wave down the valley, uprooting trees, smashing walls, sweeping away bridges and ripping up the road surface.

On the same day a man was killed nearby Kettleshulme when his car was swept off the road. He was trying to reach his wife who was out walking but quite safe. Mercifully no one was killed in Wildboarclough.

I visited the scene a few days after the event and was amazed by the extent of the devastation. After a great deal of painstaking rebuilding work, the valley is now restored to its former glory, the absence of moss on new dry stone walls being the only sign of the extensive restoration work.

Cross the bridge and take some to explore the village. On your left is the impressive facade of Crag Mill. The mill was latterly used as a post office and as such was easily the largest village post office in England. Further up the hill is a fine stone church.

Return over the bridge to the road and turn right. The immaculate row of stone cottages on your left belonged to the mill. Built from the local rose coloured Macclesfield stone with decorative arched windows they further enhance the charm and character of the village.

The road continues for four kms. through woodland and open countryside with the brook weaving from side to side under the road. This secluded and tranquil valley is in many ways reminiscent of the Lake District. After four kms. you will reach a left turn to Forest Chapel. Ignore this and continue for a further km. to a second left turn, again signed for Forest Chapel.

Forest Chapel

Turn left and then immediately right opposite a house called the Forest Lodge onto a rough track. Climb steadily for half a km. to Forest Chapel.

This tiny hillside hamlet shelters in a hollow on the side of Toot Hill. The chapel dates back to 1673 and at 400 metres is one of the highest in the country. In August each year a rush-bearing ceremony is held. This dates back to the seventeenth century when church floors were usually earth and once a year rushes were laid on the floor as a primitive sort of carpet.

POINT 3 TO POINT 1

From Forest Chapel head north west up a rough track way-marked number 3. The track climbs steadily for just over a km. following the edge of Macclesfield Forest. Behind you are marvellous views of Wildboarclough valley with Shutlingsloe, shaped like a huge hound's tooth, towering above. You will pass two large telecommunications dishes on the brow of the hill and then the track descends for half a km. to meet a metalled road. Turn left and descend steeply for a km. to Hartingland. Turn right at the T-junction and follow the lane for a further km. to Clough House Farm.

Follow the track to the right of the farm, pass through a gate and follow the track down the hill to a stream. Cross the steam and follow a track for about a km. between two reservoirs to the village of Langley.

Towering above Langley to the North is the buttress of Tegg's Nose. The hill, which supposedly derived its unusual name from the Norse god Tegga, is now a country park. A statue of Tegga lies prostrate in the car park and there is an interesting exhibition of quarry machinery on the hill itself. The views from the top of the hill are magnificent and it is well worth a visit when you have finished this bike ride. Regrettably bikes are not allowed in the park.

Turn left through the village for a km. to the Leather Smithy Inn. Turn right, follow the road around Ridgegate reservoir and the car park from which we started is half a km. further on the right.

TRAIL 16 - THE CLOUD

Distance: 18 kilometres (12 miles)

Terrain: Hilly, rough tracks, minor roads and canal towpath (permit required - see below).

Grading: Moderate.

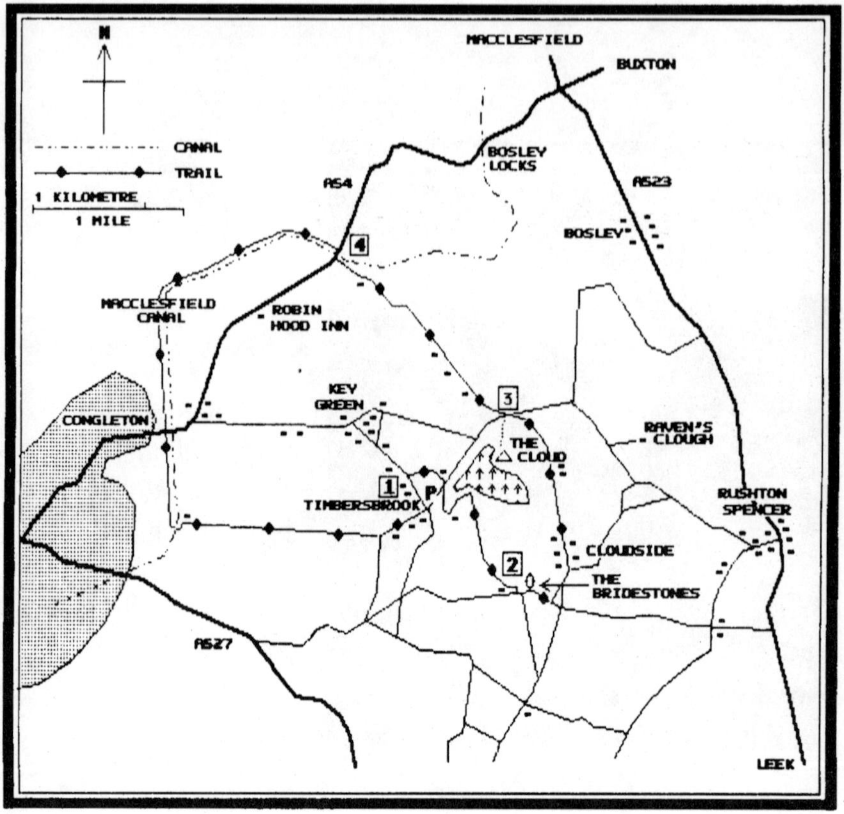

Although strictly just outside the boundaries of the National Park, I make no apologies for including this trail which includes some of the finest scenery in the area.

The Cloud is the distinctive wedge shaped peak that towers above Congleton, a busy market town on the western fringe of the Peak District. From the summit there are panoramic views of the surrounding area.

Our return journey is along the picturesque Macclesfield Canal. You need a permit to cycle along the towpath. This can be obtained for a modest charge from the British Waterways Board, Marple Locks, Marple, Cheshire. This permit is also required for Trail 18.

POINT 1

Our starting point is the sleepy village of Timbersbrook that shelters at the foot of the Cloud. Turn east for Timbersbrook off the A54 Buxton road on the northern outskirts of Congleton and follow the signs for the picnic area and car park.

POINT 1 TO POINT 2

Turn right out of the car park, continue down the road for half a km. and turn right into Acorn Lane. Follow the wooded lane uphill for half a km. until it meets a road.

Cross the road onto Gosberryhole Lane and continue upwards. After a few hundred metres, the lane bends around to the left and you will see a superb view of Congleton Edge and Mow Cop through a gap in the trees. As you climb, a footpath to the summit of the Cloud goes off to your left, marked by a National Trust sign.

Bear right and follow a tranquil wooded lane for two kms. to where it meets the road. Turn left up the road and after about two hundred metres turn left onto a driveway with a stone wall at one side. Just in front to your left are the Bridestones. These stone slabs were erected at the entrance to a neolithic burial chamber. A gate to your left allows access for you to take a closer look at this site of archaeological interest.

POINT 2 TO POINT 3

Return to the road and turn left. After half a km. turn left into a lane. Follow the lane for a short distance and turn left again towards the hamlet of Cloudside. As its name suggests, Cloudside is a group of stone buildings spread out along the side of The Cloud. Continue along the lane, passing a farm on your right and a chapel and houses on your left. The views to your right are breathtaking. The area of water you can see in the distance is Bosley reservoir.

After two kms. you will pass a lodge on your right where they practice clay pigeon shooting. Continue over the brow of a hill and descend for a km. to a crossroads. As you descend there are spectacular views over the Cheshire Plain. The viaduct below carries the main-line railway.

POINT 3 TO POINT 4

If you wish to climb the Cloud leave your bike here and follow the steep path over a stile on your left to the summit. The ascent is arduous but the views from the top are breathtaking and well worth the climb. To the west is the Cheshire Plain with the huge dish of Jodrell Bank radio telescope and the Peckforton Hills in the distance and. Looking south is the ruined folly at Mow Cop.

Eastwards you can see the rocky ridge of the Roaches and the distinctive pyramid shape of Shutlingsloe. To the north is Croker Hill with its prominent communications tower.

The Cloud From Macclesfield Canal

The summit is crowned by huge slabs of pink gritstone. If you examine the rock it contains fossilised shells and pebbles. Hardly surprising since the whole of the Cheshire Plain was once a sea bed.

One of the slabs has a large footprint shaped indentation that according to the legend, was caused by a giant striding across the hills.

Return to the road and cross over into Peover Lane. Follow the lane down for three kms. to the Buxton road by a bridge over the Macclesfield Canal.

POINT 4 TO POINT 1

Turn right over the bridge and right again through a gate onto the towpath. Head west along the tow path through idyllic countryside. After approximately six kms. you will reach a main line railway bridge. Continue along the towpath for half a km. past a metal footbridge to the next stone bridge.

Leave the canal at this point, pass over the bridge and follow Brookhouse Lane upwards for two kms. to where it meets the road. Turn left and follow the road down to Timbersbrook. Turn left in the centre of the village and then right into the car park and the end of this trail.

TRAIL 17 - RUDYARD LAKE

Distance: 18 kilometres (12 miles)

Terrain: Hilly on the return leg, disused railway line, and minor roads.

Grading: Easy.

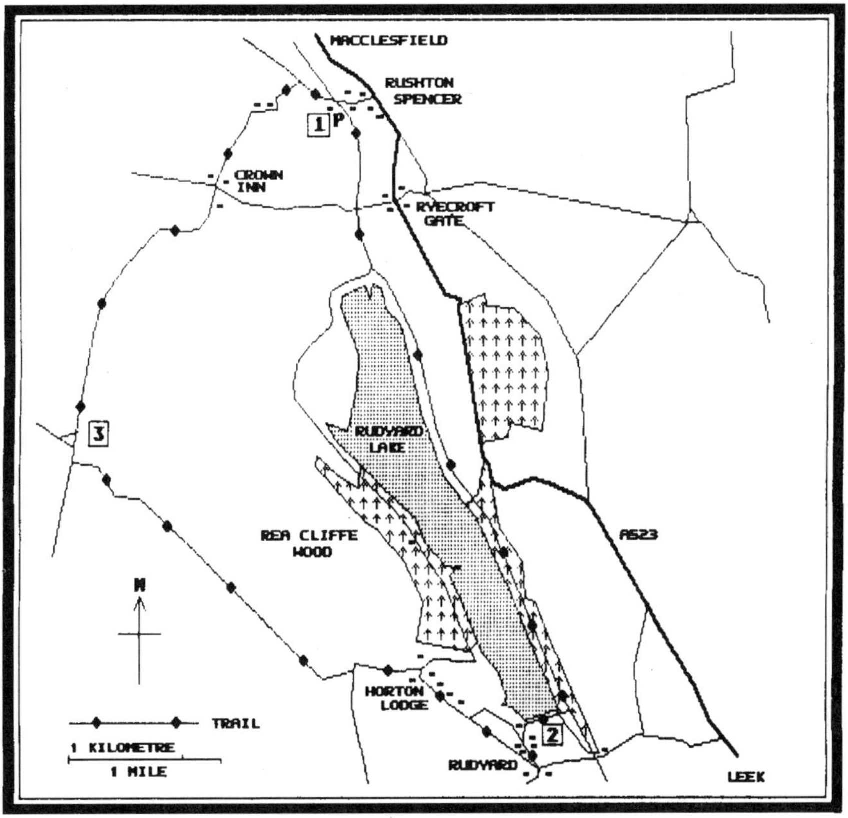

Rudyard reservoir, known locally as Rudyard Lake, was constructed in 1831 to feed the Caldon canal. It lies in a secluded valley between Macclesfield and Leek on the western edge of the National Park. The lake is popular with the sailing fraternity and with the wooded slopes on either side, the scenery is reminiscent of the Lake District.

At the end of the nineteenth century the lake was a favourite escape for a young couple, Lockwood Kipling and Alice Macdonald, from the drabness of the nearby Potteries where they lived. Lockwood asked Alice to be his wife by the lake shore, they were married and later emigrated to India. When their son was born, they named him Rudyard, after the part of England they loved so much. The son was of course the famous author Rudyard Kipling.

This trail completes a circuit of the lake using the disused Leek to Macclesfield railway line on the outward journey and returning through the lanes on the opposite shore.

POINT 1

Our starting point is a public car park adjacent to the Knott Inn in Rushton Spencer. Turn west off the A523 Macclesfield to Leek road in the centre of the village towards Woodhouse Green. The car park is on the left just after the Knott Inn.

POINT 1 TO POINT 2

Follow the disused railway track southwards from the car park for about for two kms. Shortly after passing under the road bridge the track divides. Bear left under a bridge and follow the track along the side of the lake for four kms. to the dam.

In the summer a narrow gauge railway runs alongside the track carrying visitors for lake side trips. The views from the side of the lake are superb and are only surpassed by the view from the dam that provides an uninterrupted vista down the length of the lake.

Rudyard Lake

With the boats in full sail against a backdrop of a blue sky the lake is an incomparable sight.

POINT 2 TO POINT 3

Cross the dam and pass through the gate to your left. Climb up the lane by the Rudyard Lake Hotel and turn left along the road into Rudyard village. Much of the architecture is Victorian and there is a most impressive stone war memorial by the road junction. Opposite the war memorial is the Poachers Arms, a large stone public house that makes an excellent refreshment stop.

Turn sharp right by the war memorial and climb up the hill for two kms., passing Horton Lodge school on your right. Follow the road around to the left for a km. and bear right at the next junction. The road now climbs steadily for three kms. to a T-junction. Turn left along the road and stop top admire the view.

POINT 3 TO POINT 1

The vista from this point is spectacular, taking in Rudyard Lake, the Roaches and the hills beyond. Continue along the road towards Rushton Spencer, descend steeply for three kms. and then climb up to a road junction.

Almost directly opposite is the Crown Inn and down its left hand side is a narrow lane. Take this lane and follow it for two kms., dropping steeply to the village of Rushton Spencer. Turn right and after a short distance you will arrive back at the car park and the finish of this trail.

TRAIL 18 - MIDDLEWOOD WAY AND LYME PARK

Distance: 33 kilometres (22 miles)

Terrain: Mostly level, disused railway line, minor roads, canal towpath (permit required, see below), and a short stretch of main road.

Grading: Easy.

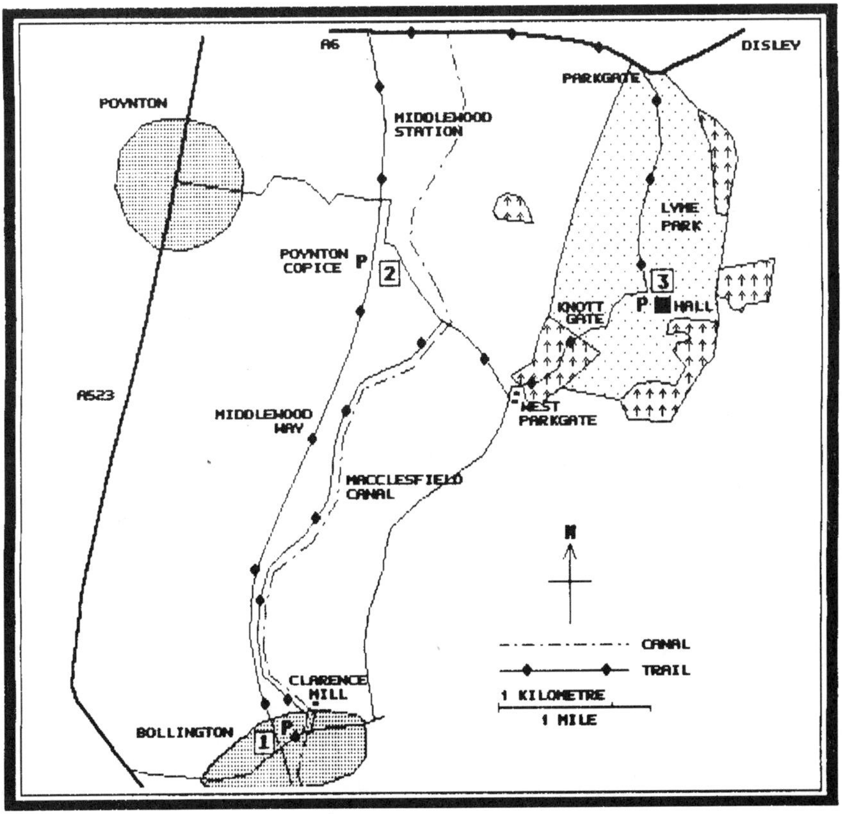

Lyme Park, home of the Leigh family since 1388, was bequeathed to the National Trust in 1946, The house, which is open to the public, is one of the finest in the Peak District and includes exquisite Elizabethan and Victorian state rooms. The grounds are equally impressive, covering some 1300 acres of park and woodland. A herd of Red Deer wander freely around the park further enhancing its natural beauty.

The outward journey to Lyme Park is along Middlewood Way, a disused railway track that runs for fifteen kms. along the edge of the Cheshire Plain between Macclesfield and Middlewood. The track was renovated by Macclesfield Borough Council in 1982 and is now used for walking, cycling and horse riding.

The return leg is along the tow path of the picturesque Macclesfield Canal, which is part of the acclaimed Cheshire Ring. You will need a permit to cycle on the towpath. This can be obtained for a modest charge from British Waterways Board, Marple Locks, Marple, Cheshire. This permit can also be used for Trail 16.

POINT 1

Our starting point is the Middlewood Way car park in Bollington. Turn east off the A523 Macclesfield to Stockport road into Bollington village. Follow the road through the village and take the first left turn after you pass under the railway viaduct. The car park is on your left at the bottom of the hill.

POINT 1 TO POINT 2

A path leads from the car park up a set of steps onto Middlewood Way. Head north along the track for approximately nine kms. to the car park at Poynton Coppice.

As you cycle along this easy track, take time to admire the panoramic views of the Cheshire Plain to the west. The cities of Stockport and Manchester can be seen to the north west and on a clear day you can see the planes taking off and landing at Manchester Airport.

POINT 2 TO POINT 3

Pass through the car park and continue along the track for three kms. to Middlewood Station where the Whaley Bridge to Stockport line crosses under Middlewood Way. A further km. brings you to the A6 at High Lane Rose Hill. Leave Middlewood Way at this point and turn right along the A6 towards Disley. Follow the road for three kms. and you will see the entrance to Lyme Park on your right. **Please note that cycling in the Park is concessionary and you must give precedence to pedestrians and keep to the route indicated in this book.**

As you pass through the entrance, the magnificent grounds open up before you. The driveway now leads for three kms. through lush parkland to Lyme Hall. The prominent square stone tower on your left is a watch tower called the 'Cage' that was built in the fifteenth century. As you ride through the park watch out for the Red Deer. When you reach the Hall I strongly recommend that you spend time exploring the house and gardens before you continue.

The Hall itself dates back to the sixteenth century but has been extended and renovated several times. The impressive Palladian style architecture was added by a Venetian architect in the eighteenth century. The Hall contains many art treasures, including a portrait of the Black Prince and some of the finest tapestries and wood carvings in England. Extensive gardens surround the Hall and provide a splendid setting for this magnificent building.

POINT 3 TO POINT 1

From the car park by the Hall follow the driveway westwards, up and over a hill to the Knott Gate.

Lyme Hall

Pass through the gate and follow the track down through a delightful wooded glade for about a km. to the West Parkgate. Turn left along a track for a short way and then right down the road. After about a km. the road passes through a tunnel under the canal. At the far end of the tunnel turn immediately right up the steps to the canal towpath.

From this point the return journey is straightforward, following the towpath for about nine kms. back to Bollington. This is a route of much scenic beauty and great tranquillity where the narrowboats make gentle progress along the canal.

As you enter Bollington you will see the huge edifice of Clarence Mill on the opposite bank, a monument to a bygone era when Bollington was an important cotton town. Leave the canal at this point and drop down a lane to the road. Turn right down the road and right again before the railway viaduct. Descend the hill and turn left into the car park from which we started.

TRAIL 19 - THE LONGNOR CIRCUIT

Distance: 15 kilometres (10 miles)

Terrain: Hilly, bridleways, rough tracks and minor roads.

Grading: Moderate.

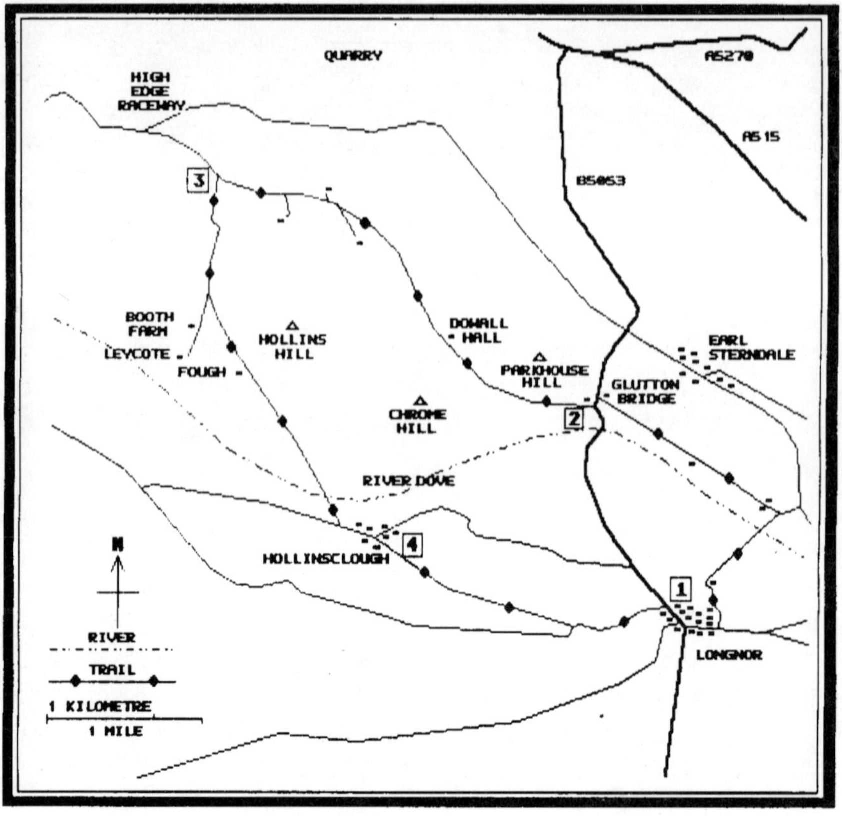

No tour of the Peak District would be complete without a visit to Longnor. The village is perched on the ridge that separates the magnificent Dove and Manifold valleys. Longnor is a tightly packed collection of stone buildings and cobbled streets. Walking through its streets is like stepping back in time. In the centre of the village is a market square and the splendid market hall (1873), which is now a craft shop. A sign above the entrance gives a list of the tolls payable to the Lord of the Manor on market days; fourpence from the sellers for a pen of sheep or pigs; a penny from the buyer of a pig.

At the rear of the market square is a fine stone church. Built in 1780, the church yard contains the grave of William Billinge who is reputed to have lived to the ripe old age of 112 years. According to legend he was a soldier for over sixty years and fought in many of the country's great battles. The secret of his longevity was apparently that he never smoked or drank. Living in Longnor must have been a terrible temptation for him since there are four pubs in the village centre.

POINT 1

The trail starts from the centre of the village. Turn south off the A515 Buxton to Ashbourne road at Brierlow Bar. Follow the B5053 for nine kms. to Longnor and park in the market square.

POINT 1 TO POINT 2

With your back to the market hall head left along the road towards Crowdecote. Turn left up a lane by the last house on the left at the edge of the village. Follow the lane up the hill and onto a bridleway. The bridleway descends the other side of the hill into the Dove Valley and passes around the left hand side of a barn.

Follow the bridleway across the fields for a km. to a bridge. To your left there are two distinctive peaks that look as if a hill has been split in half.

The Market Square - Longnor

These are Chrome and Parkhouse hills. Cross the bridge and half a km. along a broad grassy lane brings you to a rough track. Turn left, follow the track through a farm yard and continue along the Dove Valley, passing through several gates. The track is level and makes very pleasant cycling. After one and a half kms. you will reach the road at Glutton Bridge.

POINT 2 TO POINT 3

Turn left and then immediately right, before the river bridge, into a lane. This lane leads along a superb valley between Chrome Hill and Parkhouse Hill. Their limestone crags tower above the green pasture and a stream meanders alongside the lane. This delightful setting continues for one and a half kms. to Dowall Farm. The lane now enters a limestone gorge and climbs for a km. to emerge through a gate onto a high plateau. Cross the plateau for one and a half kms., passing a limestone track on your left. At the far end of the plateau you will cross the brow of a hill and arrive at a junction by a cattle grid. The road ahead leads to High Edge Raceway, a venue for stock car racing. Our route is to your left along a minor road.

POINT 3 TO POINT 4

Follow the road that winds down a hillside for almost a km. towards Booth Farm. Just before the farm, bear left onto a limestone track and follow it along the hillside to a house called Fough. Bear left by the house and follow a bridleway down the hillside for a km. Cross a bridge over the infant river Dove and climb for half a km. to meet a road. Turn left and you arrive at the village of Hollinsclough.

POINT 4 TO POINT 1

Carry straight on through the village and follow the road for three kms. to a T-junction. Turn left and after half a km. turn right towards Longnor. A short descent brings you back to our starting point.

TRAIL 20 - THE MERMAID AND MORRIDGE

Distance: 40 kilometres (27 miles)

Terrain: Hilly, minor roads and bridleways.
Note: This trail covers long stretches of grass and should be avoided in wet weather.

Grading Difficult.

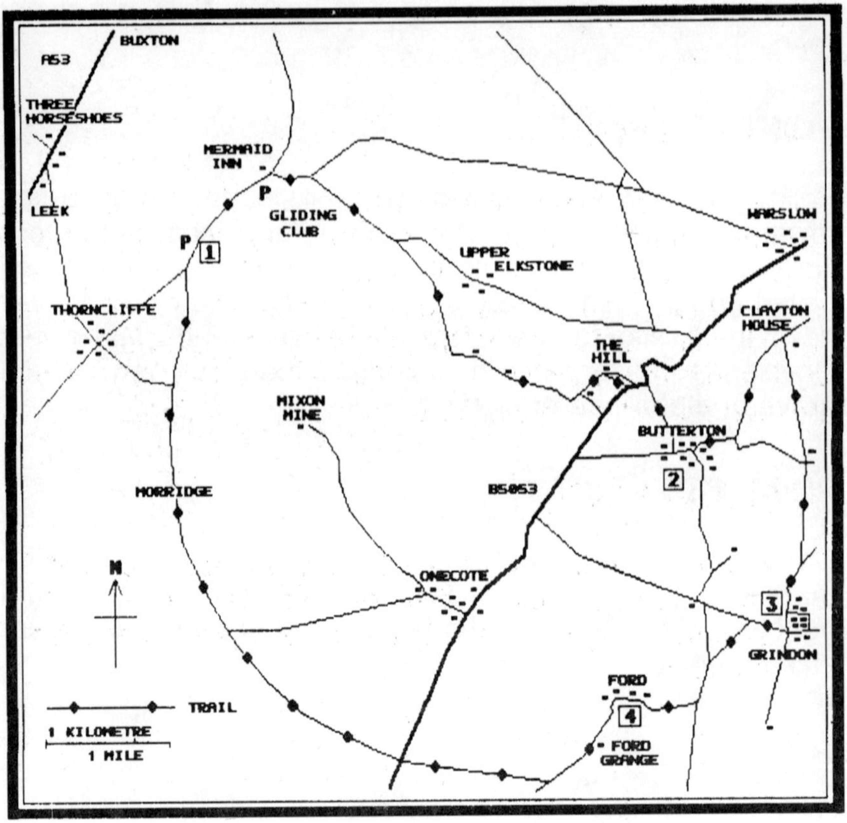

The Mermaid Inn is perched high on a gritstone ridge called Morridge that forms the south west boundary of the National Park. Built over two hundred years ago, the Mermaid is full of character and makes an excellent refreshment stop after your bike ride.

The Mermaid On Morridge

From its elevated position the Mermaid has commanding views over the surrounding countryside. To the north the jagged black rocks of Hen Cloud, the Roaches and Ramshaw Rocks erupt from the heather landscape.

Westwards is the fertile valley around Meerbrook where Tittesworth reservoir shimmers like a brilliant jewel. Our route lies south where the moorland falls away to the undulating limestone hills around the Manifold Valley.

Taking advantage of air currents convecting up the edge, Staffordshire Gliding Club have sited their aerodrome directly opposite the Mermaid. You can watch these graceful craft sweeping into the air and spiralling silently skywards.

In addition to agriculture, the local economy around Morridge was supplemented during the eighteenth and nineteenth century by the income from copper mining. Mixon mines on the eastern flank of Morridge operated until 1870 when the competition from the large copper mine at nearby Ecton, owned by the Duke of Devonshire, became to great.

POINT 1

Our starting point is a small road-side car park on Morridge, one km. south west of the Mermaid. Turn east off the A53 Buxton to Leek road towards Thorncliffe by the Three Horseshoes Inn on Blackshaw Moor. Follow the road for just over a km. to Thorncliffe. Turn left up the hill for two kms. The car park is on your left at the top of the hill.

POINT 1 TO POINT 2

From the car park, head north east towards the Mermaid Inn, taking in the superb views to your left. Turn right opposite the inn skirt the perimeter of the gliding club and turn right again for Elkstone. Follow the road along Royledge for one and a half kms. to where the road divides.

Bear right and continue along the edge for two kms. The lane turns sharp right by a gate leading to Cave Farm. The extensive views from this point encompass the Manifold and Dove valleys and are simply superb. A prominent needle shaped church spire on the plain below will catch your eye. This is at Butterton - our next point of call.

Follow the lane down the hillside through farmyards and several metal gates. At the bottom of the hill the lane turns right through a metal gate by a farm on your right. Carry straight on along a rough track for half a km. towards The Hill Farm. Just before the farm turn right onto a bridleway and climb up the hill for half a km. to the B5053. Turn left for a few hundred metres and then right for Butterton and the Manifold valley. A further km. brings you to the charming village of Butterton.

The village is a compact collection of stone buildings crowded on a sheltered western slope. Bearing left at the junction and then left again at the next takes you through the village to the church. Built in 1871 its magnificent spire is one of the finest in the Peak District. If you are hungry or thirsty you can sample the excellent food and drink at the Black Lion Inn that is on your right.

POINT 2 TO POINT 3

Follow the road to the left of the church and bear left at junction on the edge of the village. Continue down this ro for two kms. and watch for a bridleway sign on the righ Clayton House. Turn right onto the bridleway and bear ri Clayton House onto a limestone track. Follow the track a a field and bear right off the track and through a wooden gate just before a cattle grid.

Cross the field to a gate and follow the hedge down to another gate in the bottom left hand corner of the next field. Cross a stream and head up the hill to a gate directly opposite. Bear slightly right across the field to a gate in the top right hand corner. Follow the hedge on your left through two gates to Wallacre Farm. Carry straight on through three wooden gates to a road.

Cross the road, pass through a metal gate and follow the right hand hedge down to a muddy gateway. From this point you can see the top of the church spire at Grindon that is our next destination. To your left is the picturesque Manifold Valley. Continue to follow the hedge and descend steeply to Hoo Brook. Cross two bridges and bear left onto the bridleway for Grindon. The bridleway climbs steeply to a gate. Ossoms Hill to your left overlooks the Manifold Valley and is owned by the National Trust. Continue your ascent, following the right hand hedge through a narrow wooden gate and then to a wide gate. Cross the brow of the hill to meet a lane. If you look to your left you will see the limestone buttress of Thors Cave in the Manifold Valley. Our route is to the right, along the lane for a km. to Grindon.

POINT 3 TO POINT 4

This ancient settlement was recorded in the Domesday Book. The name Grindon is derived from Grendon that means "green hill". As you enter the village you pass the magnificent All Saints Church. Gothic in design and similar to the church at Butterton, the church was built in 1848 and has a superb needle spire. The previous church on this site - The Chapel Of Ilam - was built in the eleventh century and destroyed by fire in the nineteenth century. The village pub is the Cavalier Inn that used to be a smithy and makes an excellent stop for efreshments.

From the church, continue past the children's playground and turn right. Turn right at the next junction (turn left if you are visiting the Cavalier Inn), follow the road for half a km. and turn left towards Waterhouses and Ashbourne. Follow the road for a km. to a T-junction. Turn left, continue along this road for a km. and take the turning on your right to Ford.

Drop down the hill for a km. through a wooded glade into the enchanting hamlet of Ford, a charming group of farm buildings and houses clustered around the river Hamps.

POINT 4 TO POINT 1

Cross the bridge and follow the road for two kms. past Ford Grange to a crossroads. Turn right for one and a half kms. to meet the B5053. Take the road almost directly opposite, for Bradnot and Blakemere, onto the escarpment of Morridge. You now climb for ten kms. along the backbone of this moorland edge. The spectacular views more than compensate for the drudge of the ascent. At the end of your climb turn right at the junction and the car park we started from is just on your left.